Greek Mythology for Teens

Enthralling Tales and Myths from Ancient Greece

Free limited time bonus

Stop for a moment. We have a free bonus set up for you. The problem is this: we forget 90% of everything that we read after 7 days. Crazy fact, right? Here's the solution: we've created a printable, 1-page pdf summary for this book that you're reading now. All you have to do to get your free pdf summary is to go to the following website: **https://livetolearn.lpages.co/enthrallinghistory/**

Once you do, it will be intuitive. Enjoy, and thank you!

Table of Contents

Introduction

About Ancient Greek Society and Mythology

Greek myths have captured our imagination for millennia. Though these stories are set thousands of years ago and feature godly beings and mystical monsters, these tales still manage to be relatable. That is because myths were used to explain the unexplainable. The ancients used myths to explain why the seasons changed or why volcanoes erupted. Myths also explain why we fall in love with those we cannot be with or why we grieve the dead.

That being said, myths are also rooted in their place and culture of origin. To better appreciate these incredible stories, it is helpful to know more about the society that birthed them.

So, let's start at the beginning.

The ones we now call "ancient Greeks" were known as the Hellenes during their time. Their nation, Hellas, expanded far beyond the borders of today's modern nation of Greece. They lived across the Mediterranean Sea, with cities spreading from Turkey all the way to Spain.[1] So while we understand them to have been part of the same people and to have shared many cultural similarities, there were many regional differences in their belief systems, their civic laws, and their traditions.

---

[1] (John, McNab and Sullivan 2013)

However, it is important to remember that our knowledge of the ancient Greeks is incredibly flawed. By putting together evidence found in archaeological sites, surviving manuscripts, and myths, we can make educated guesses about their world. But those guesses are still just that—guesses. Much knowledge about that time has been lost forever due to things being forgotten, misplaced, or purposefully destroyed. That lost knowledge cannot be recovered, which means the puzzle we try to create will forever be missing crucial pieces.[2]

We must also keep in mind our sources. Until very recently, academics had different standards for what it meant to record something accurately. It was not uncommon for scholars to come up with elaborate narratives or theories from very little evidence. This is how many misconceptions and misinformation about the past are passed down and continue to endure even when they are proven to be wrong. For this reason, we must remember that there is a high possibility that the myths we know today are very different from the myths the ancient Greeks knew.

All of this aside, as far as we can tell, it does appear that the extent of the ancient Greeks' geographical knowledge was focused on the Mediterranean Sea. This is very clearly reflected in their mythology, as we see heroes traveling from Greece to North Africa, Turkey, and Italy. Early on, the Greeks might have even believed that Mount Olympus, the seat of their gods, was the center of the world.[3]

They divided their history into five distinct ages, each of them getting progressively worse than the one that preceded it. These five ages were:

- The Golden Age
- The Silver Age
- The Bronze Age
- The Heroic Age
- The Iron Age

Except for the creation myth in Chapter 1, the myths in this book all tend to fall within the Heroic Age. They are believed to have been first recorded and popularized during the Iron Age.

---

[2] (Illes 2009)

[3] (Bulfinch 2013)

This division of time may be reflective of ancient Greek history. Current historians have divided their timeline into the following periods:

- Ancient Greece (dating as far back as 3000 BCE)
- Mycenean Greece (from 1400 to 1150 BCE)
- Greek Dark Ages (from 1100 to 700 BCE)
- Archaic Greece (700 to 450 BCE)
- Classical Greece (510 to 323 BCE)

Most scholars agree that Mycenean Greece roughly corresponds to the Heroic Age and that the grand myths of the era might have been based on real events. It is disputable whether Achilles, Helen of Troy, and the famed Trojan Horse really existed. However, historians *do* know that Troy was a real city, and they believe the Trojan War to have been a real conflict. The ancient Greeks did not see history as separate from fantasy, and they preferred to interweave fact and fiction to create compelling narratives about their people, cities, and culture.[4]

About this Book

We will begin this book with the ancient Greek origin myth, from the creation of the universe to the Olympians' rise to power. After that, we will explore the most famous narrative of four famous Greek heroes: Theseus, Perseus, Herakles, and Jason. Finally, our last story will be that of the famed House of Atreus.

Selecting which myths to include in this book was a difficult process. To narrow down our list, we focused on stories about mortal heroes or demigods. You will enjoy heroic tales of adventure and dark conflicts. If you find these myths to be interesting, we highly recommend you seek out others. The other myths are just as fascinating; we simply had to exclude some because we had limited space to work with and wanted our stories to have common themes tying them together.

We ask you to remember that there is a myriad of variations to these myths. Whenever one chooses to tell these stories, they are making an editorial decision regarding which version they will include. When possible, we tried to include information on these differences without ruining the reading experience.

---

[4] (John, McNab and Sullivan 2013)

Content Warning

Finally, before we begin, there's a final but very important note to keep in mind.

This book is not a retelling of Greek mythology. We are not seeking to recontextualize these stories the way a novelist would, and we are not seeking to examine them through an academic lens like a scholar. We are simply telling the stories as they were. However, it would be irresponsible of us not to acknowledge that many of these tales contain elements that are problematic to a modern audience or may be triggering to certain readers.

Many gods engaged in sexual intercourse with women through deception. For example, they would disguise themselves as their husbands and have sex with them. At the time, such actions would likely not be viewed as harshly. Today, we would understand these gods to have committed rape. That is not to excuse their actions by claiming it was a different time. Regardless of whether it was viewed as socially acceptable or not, these actions would have been as wrong then as they are now. However, understanding that these would not have been considered rape from a *cultural* perspective helps us understand why certain characters who come across as evil do not get punished for their evil deeds.

It is also important to note that in these myths, a "hero" is not necessarily a "good person." This is not due solely to the shifting moral values we specified above but due to the ancient Greeks preferring their heroes to be flawed. Sometimes, they did despicable actions and faced the consequences for their errors.

We ask you to keep in mind cultural differences and how they might have played into the actions of these heroes. While it may seem silly to be furious at someone for not properly welcoming someone into their home, hospitality was seen as sacred to the ancient Greeks. Failing to properly honor one's guest or host was punishable by law. Also, while stories today preach about how revenge is never the answer, back when these stories took place, vengeance was viewed as one's moral duty. Failure to take revenge against someone who had wronged you would be viewed as shameful.

We chose to tell these stories while remaining as true to the myth as possible, but we must also acknowledge the presence of these issues and why certain readers might be uncomfortable with them.

Chapter 1: Birth of the Cosmos and the Wars That Followed

At the beginning of time, Chaos ruled the universe. There was nothing besides it, nothing beyond it. Empty yet vast, this unfathomable force is the origin of everything we know, everything that existed, and everything that will ever exist.

But then, two children came into being: Erebus, the Darkness, and Nyx, the Night. Together, Darkness and Night created Brightness and Day, Aether and Hemera. These two brought light into existence, setting forth the beginning of time.

Nyx had many children. According to some, she created those on her own, and they emerged from her just as Nyx and Erebus emerged from Chaos. There were the twins, Thanatos, Peaceful Death, and Hypnos, Sleep. While both lived in the underworld, Hypnos was said to reside in a poppy-filled cave by the River Lethe (the River of Forgetfulness). Thanatos was said to be hated by people, and he hated them in return. In the underworld, the Moirai—the Three Fates (Clotho, Lachesis, and Atropos)—spun and weaved the threads of destiny. Their powers were greater than all other gods. There was also Charon, the Ferryman; the Keres, death spirits; Momus, or Blame; and Geras, who was Old Age. There was Eris, who was Strife, and Nemesis, who was Retribution. And there were many, many others.

Then came Gaea, Mother Earth and the mother of all life. And with her came Tartarus, a being who was both a deity and an abyss of eternal punishment and suffering. Just as Nyx bore many children, Gaea also spawned offspring that would help shape the cosmos. Ouranos, the Sky, was one of many.

During those times, relations were ill-defined. The familial bonds that tie deities together cannot be compared to the ones we share as humans. The Earth and Sky were mother and son, but they were also lovers. Twelve new deities were born from their union, and these children were known as the Titans.

The six male children were known by the names of Oceanus, Crius, Hyperion, Coeus, Iapetus, and Cronus. The six female children were known as Theia, Mnemosyne, Phoebe, Themis, Tethys, and Rhea.

Gaea and Ouranos were happy, and their children prospered. But things changed, and the love they shared soured into hatred. As the story goes, after the Titans, Gaea gave birth to three monstrous beings known as Hecatonchieres. They were giants who had fifty different heads and one hundred different arms.

Some say that when Ouranos saw these three hideous creatures, he was so disgusted that he thrust them back into Gaea's womb, causing her an indescribable amount of pain. Others say that he locked the Hecatonchieres up in Tartarus, breaking poor Gaea's heart. Regardless of which version of the tale you believe, the result remains the same. By rejecting the Hecatonchieres, Ouranos hurt Gaea. And she hated him.

"He'll pay for what he's done," Gaea whispered to herself. "He'll regret ever hurting my children."

And so, Gaea went to her other kids, the Titans, and searched for who would be willing to take on their father.

Only Cronus, the youngest of the Titans, answered his mother's call.

"In return for your help, you can rule in his place," Gaea promised him.

"Thank you, Mother," Cronus said. "I will do you proud."

Together, they came up with a plan. Gaea gave her son a sickle that she crafted out of a large stone and then told him to hide. When Ouranos appeared, she distracted him through seduction. Ouranos was so focused on the woman in his arms that he did not hear Cronus creep up behind them. He did not realize what was happening until he felt a sharp stab in his shoulder.

Gaea stepped back, a smirk appearing on her lips. She watched as Cronus tackled his father to the ground. Finally, when victory was all but secure, Cronus took the sickle to Ouranos's genitals and castrated him.

Ouranos screamed, and Cronus reigned victorious. Just as the new ruler was about to banish his father to the depths of Tartarus, the fallen deity spoke up.

"Mark my words, son. Just as you have attacked me, your son will attack you. Just as you have overthrown me, your son shall overthrow you. Just as you banish and imprison me, your son shall banish and imprison you."

Cronus only scoffed at his father and sent him away.

From the blood of Ouranos that soaked the ground, the three Erinyes or the Furies—Alecto, Megara, and Tisophone—were created. Ouranos's genitals were thrown into the ocean. It is said that when it mixed with the seafoam, it created Aphrodite, the goddess of love and beauty. The Hecatonchieres were freed, though only temporarily.

And so, the Golden Age began. Cronus took Rhea, his sister, as his wife. Prometheus, the son of Iapetus, created humans out of clay. This was a time of harmony and happiness, with humanity and gods living together side by side.

But as you might have already learned, things always change. Peace hardly ever lasts.

After years and years, Rhea finally became pregnant with a child. Happiness bloomed inside her, as she was eager to become a mother and have a child to love. But Ouranos's curse rang inside Cronus's head, and paranoia began to take hold of him.

Finally, it came time for the baby to be born. Her name was Hestia, and she was to become the goddess of the hearth, domestic peace, the home, and family. She would have the sweetest temperament of all the gods. She was a peacekeeper to the core, a gentle girl who would always care for her family.

Rhea loved her baby girl when she held her in her arms. She was her first child, and Rhea thought she would be a wonderful sister and goddess to humanity.

But Cronus could not let Hestia live. He took her from Rhea's arms and devoured the baby girl, ignoring their cries.

"What have you done?" Rhea demanded, crying. Her arms felt empty without her daughter.

"I will not have any child threaten my rule," Cronus said. "You do not need any children."

Cronus carrying away one of his children.

And perhaps that would have been the end of things. But Rhea fell pregnant again. She had another baby girl, Demeter, who became the goddess of harvest and crops. Demeter was humble and good. She would become compassionate, emotional, caring, and adored.

Rhea tried to fight back, but yet again, Cronus took the baby girl from her arms and ate her whole. Rhea wasn't sure how she could possibly handle this much grief.

She fell pregnant again with yet another baby girl. Hera was to be the goddess of marriage and of married women. Strong-willed, she had the temperament of a queen and would never let bad deeds go unpunished.

"Please, not my little Hera!" Rhea cried. "She'll do you no harm! I promise to keep her far away from you!"

But Cronus would not listen. And once more, he ate his daughter, showing her no mercy.

When Rhea fell pregnant again, she gave birth to a boy. Hades was his name, and he would become the king of the dead and the god of the underworld. Even as a babe, Hades was brooding and serious, but he was not evil or unkind. He was beloved by his mother, but that would not be enough to save him.

Next came another boy. Poseidon was his name, and he was to be the god of the seas and storms. He could be tranquil one moment and screaming the next. Poseidon had the kind of temperament one could not ignore, as he was born to rule over the waves of the ocean. Cronus also showed him no mercy.

When Rhea fell pregnant for the sixth time, she knew she could not handle losing yet another child. She could not go through this pain again. So, when her sixth child was born—another boy—she didn't hold him like she did his older siblings. Instead, she hid him immediately. She then reached for a bean-shaped rock and bundled it in sheets and blankets.

Cronus marched toward her. He took the rock from her arms, thinking it to be his sixth child. Rhea screamed and pleaded just as she did before, even though she knew her true child was safe. Without glancing at what he held in his hand, Cronus swallowed the rock, believing himself to have eaten yet another one of his children.

A painted frieze of Rhea giving the rock to Cronus. Painted by Karl Friedrich Schinkel.
https://commons.wikimedia.org/wiki/File:Cronos_and_Rhea_by_Karl_Friedrich_Schinkel.jpg

When Cronus left, Rhea ran to where she hid her baby boy. His name was Zeus, and he was to be the god of the sky and the god of thunder. With the sole exception of the three Fates, no being would ever be as powerful as he, and he would one day rule all living creatures and gods.

But at this point in our tale, he was only a babe. Though Rhea would have given anything to keep her one surviving child with her, she knew it would not be safe for Zeus. And so, she ran to her mother, begging her for help.

"Please! Oh, please, Mother. Find a way to protect Zeus," Rhea cried. "You know what it is like to have your husband hurt your children. Don't let Cronus take him."

Gaea listened to her daughter's pleas and agreed to help. She instructed her to take Zeus to Mount Ida in Crete.

Rhea did as her mother instructed, saying goodbye to her baby boy before returning to her cruel husband's side. She did not have any children after Zeus, and she never told Cronus that his last son was still alive.

At Mount Ida, Zeus was surrounded by tender, nurturing nymphs, female nature deities that were often anchored to specific locations. Amalthea was said to be his main foster mother. While some claim she took the form of a human woman, others claim she took the form of a sacred goat who nursed Zeus. Adamathea was a nymph who helped rear him. And when Zeus grew up, Metis, daughter of Tethys, became his teacher.

During Zeus's youth, Rhea came to visit him whenever she could. The young god would always greet his mother with open arms and a smile, eager to hear stories from her. It was through these stories that Zeus learned about his older siblings and why his father had so cruelly eaten them.

"It is I. I'm the one Ouranos warned Cronus about," Zeus thought. "And he was right. For what he's done to my siblings, I'll overthrow him and banish him to the depths of Tartarus and rule in his place."

Finally, it came time for Zeus to get his revenge. With his mother's help, he disguised himself as Cronus's cupbearer and infiltrated Mount Othrys.

The first time Zeus beheld his father, his heart was filled with rage. Zeus wanted to strike right then and there, but he knew he should bide his time. He would not be able to overthrow Cronus by himself.

Cronus did not recognize Zeus as his own and barely paid the young god any attention. This gave Zeus the opportunity to slip a special potion into his father's cup, one made of mustard and wine. The concoction was given to him by Metis.

"This potion will not kill Cronus. That is something you must do yourself," Metis said. "But this will let you accomplish your goal, and it will give you enough time to flee somewhere safe and gather your forces."

And so, after Zeus had established himself in Mount Othrys, he waited for the opportune moment. Cronus and Rhea were alone as they dined, and Zeus stood behind his father, waiting. When Rhea gave him a slight nod, Zeus approached Cronus.

"More wine, my lord?"

"Yes," Cronus said without even looking at the young cupbearer. "Fill my cup. That is your job, is it not?"

Zeus poured Metis's concoction into the cup. He held his breath as he watched his father drink it. For a few moments, nothing happened, and dread filled Zeus as he wondered if he and his mother had been betrayed by their friend.

But then, Cronus began to retch. He stood from his chair, feeling sicker than ever before. Rhea and Zeus watched in anticipation. Cronus retched again, then again. Then, finally, he vomited.

Poseidon was the first to come out, followed by Hades. Then came the girls: Hera, Demeter, and Hestia. All five of them were fully grown, and they looked at their little brother, who had also become their older brother, in awe.

"We do not have time for celebrations," Zeus said. He pointed at Cronus, who was unconscious. "We must go before he awakes. Then we must prepare for war."

"We'll follow you, brother," said the five gods. "Lead the way."

All six of the gods and Rhea fled Mount Othrys before Cronus awakened. They made Mount Olympus their new home, and they became known as the Olympians.

For the war to come, the Olympians recruited as many allies as they could. They secured the help of the Cyclops, who held no love for Cronus, and Aphrodite, who resided in Cyprus and was promised a throne on Olympus. The three Hecatonchieres, whom Cronus had imprisoned again, joined the Olympians, crafting their weapons and giving Zeus his famed lightning bolt.

Once Cronus realized what happened, he gathered his own forces as well. He called on the Titans and their children. All but Rhea, Themis, and Themis' son with Iapetus, Prometheus, joined his cause. Atlas was made commander of Cronus's army, and they made Mount Othrys their stronghold.

For ten years, the battle between the Olympians and Titans continued. Neither side relented, and neither side showed mercy. This long war became known as the Titanomachy. During that time, Zeus had five children: Athena, Hephaestus, Ares, Apollo, and Artemis. With the exception of Hephaestus, who had been cast out of Olympus by his mother, Hera, all the other godly children joined their father in the conflict.

The Olympians came out victorious. The Titans were punished for their actions. They were banished to the depths of Tartarus. Atlas was the notable exception. Because of his role as commander, he was given the burden of carrying the sky on his shoulders. The Third Order began, and with it, the Golden Age came to an end, giving rise to the Silver Age. Rhea retired from leadership, though she remained beloved by all and was often called upon for her wisdom. Zeus and his brothers split the realms between them, with Zeus ruling over the sky, Poseidon over the sea, and Hades over the dead. Earth would belong to men and be a neutral ground between them.

Activity 1: Matching Activity

Match the names in Column A with the correct attributes in Column B

Column A	Column B
Nyx	The personification of Earth
Hypnos	Mother of Zeus and five other Olympians
Cronus	Commander of Cronus's army
Rhea	The personification of the night
Hestia	Goddess of the harvest
Poseidon	God of sleep
Demeter	The Titans' seat of power
Atlas	Gaea's son and husband
Mount Othrys	Father of Zeus, husband of Rhea, son of Gaea
Ouranos	Goddess of the hearth
Gaea	God of the sea and storms

Chapter 2: Theseus and the Minotaur

As is often the case with heroes, Theseus's most famous story begins not with Theseus himself but with the actions of the enemies he would one day face.

Minos was the king of Crete, and his kingdom was prosperous. But to secure his hold on the throne so that his brothers would not take it, he prayed to the gods for recognition.

Poseidon, king of the seas and the god of storms and earthquakes, answered Minos's prayers. He sent Minos a great white bull known as the Cretan Bull (in other myths, it is known as the Marathonian Bull) under the explicit condition that the majestic creature would be sacrificed to Poseidon.

Minos's kingship had been properly recognized, and it came time for Minos to fulfill his end of the bargain and sacrifice the great white bull to the god of the seas. But Minos was proud, and he saw how many regarded his bull with admiration. How could he possibly sacrifice such a magnificent animal that earned him envious looks? No, he could not do it. His only choice was to trick Poseidon by killing one of his other bulls in hopes the god would not know the difference.

Tricking the gods is a dangerous thing. Though powerful beyond mortal imagination, they are also vindictive and easy to offend. Few things insult them more than a mortal believing they can outsmart or outdo them in any way.

Poseidon decided that if the king took so much pride in how coveted his Cretan Bull was, then this coveting should be his punishment. Poseidon asked Aphrodite, the goddess of love, to cast a spell on Minos's wife, Queen Pasiphae.

And so it was that Queen Pasiphae fell in love with the great Cretan Bull. She sought his company, and she became pregnant with the Cretan Bull's child. Eventually, she gave birth to the half-man and half-bull creature known as the Minotaur.

How the ancient Greeks depicted the Minotaur.
© Marie-Lan Nguyen / Wikimedia Commons;
https://commons.wikimedia.org/wiki/File:Tondo_Minotaur_London_E4_MAN.jpg

Minos was horrified and ashamed. He sought help from Daedalus, who was regarded as the greatest and wisest artisan, architect, and inventor the world has ever seen. The man finally told Minos he could build a giant prison composed of long, confusing paths. This would be known as the Labyrinth, and the Minotaur would live within its walls.

Minos agreed that this would be the ideal solution to his problem. He tasked Daedalus with designing the Labyrinth. Once it was complete, the Minotaur was released into it.

Years and years passed since the Minotaur's birth, and Crete entered a conflict with the great city of Athens. During the conflict, King Minos's son, Androgeus, was brutally killed. Athens ended up losing to Crete.

Minos was filled with grief and the desire for vengeance. He decided he would punish the entire city for the untimely death of his young son.

"Seven boys and seven maidens shall be sent to Crete as tribute," Minos declared. "They'll be put inside the Labyrinth and be at the Minotaur's mercy."

Athens and its people suffered through this horrific cruelty twice. Seven boys and seven maidens were chosen on two separate occasions. They were sent to the island of Crete and placed in the dark Labyrinth. These Athenian youths roamed the winding passages, unable to escape. They knew they might run into the Minotaur at any moment and meet a bloody, painful death.

When it came time for the third tribute to be sent, Prince Theseus decided that his people would no longer be terrorized by Minos and his monster.

Theseus was a son of Poseidon, though his conception was done through deception. When Aethra's husband, King Aegeus, went to make a sacrifice to the god Poseidon on their wedding night, Poseidon disguised himself as the groom and went to Aethra's bed. From this deceptive union came Theseus, who was raised and loved by King Aegeus as if he were his own flesh and blood.

"Let me go along with the next tributes, Father," Theseus asked of King Aegeus. "I'll face the monster inside the Labyrinth and put an end to the horrors inflicted on our people by King Minos!"

Like any good parent, King Aegeus was hesitant to give his son his blessing to go on this quest. He wished to protect his boy and keep him safe from harm in their beautiful city. But he also knew that as king of Athens, he could not let his people endure this cruelty any longer. He knew his son was strong and capable, and he knew that Theseus had made up his mind and would do what he believed to be right and just.

"Are you certain you wish to do this, my son?"

"Yes," Theseus said. "I'll go with the seven maidens and the six boys, and I shall bring every single one of them back to Athens alive."

"Very well, then. I give you my blessing to go through with your plan," Aegeus said. "But I first need you to promise me something."

"Anything, Father."

"Your ship will depart to Crete under black sails. When you're returning, if you survived this mission, switch the sails to white ones so we know about your victory as soon as you appear on the horizon. That way, we do not have to wait for you to reach shore to hear the news."

"Of course, Father. You have my word," Theseus said. Then, he jokingly added, "This way, you'll be able to have a celebratory feast ready when we arrive."

Aegeus smiled and patted his young son on the shoulder. "That's right, my boy."

And so, when it came time for the third set of tributes to be sent to Crete, Prince Theseus joined the seven maidens and six boys, all of whom huddled around their prince, fearful for their fate. Theseus was not afraid. He looked at the horizon with determination, fire burning in his eyes when the island of Crete finally came into sight.

Theseus and the other thirteen tributes were escorted to their cells almost immediately. However, the little time they spent outside of their cells was enough for Princess Ariadne to catch sight of the Athenian hero and fall in love with him.

Ariadne visited Theseus in his cell. Theseus saw this as an opportunity to help him on his quest. He indulged Ariadne, talking to her and endearing himself to the princess.

"I know I can defeat the Minotaur without trouble," Theseus said. "My worry is being able to get out of the Labyrinth."

Ariadne thought about the matter.

"Father had Daedalus design and construct the Labyrinth. Supposedly, no one should be able to navigate its winding, dark passages," Ariadne said. "But if one were to know how to do it, it would be Daedalus himself."

Ariadne looked at Theseus's handsome face. She did not want her beloved to die, yet she knew that if she went through with her plan, it would mean turning her back on her father, her mother, and her entire city. She had to choose between saving Theseus and those thirteen other young Athenians and her life as she knew it.

I grieve the loss of my brother, Androgeus, Ariadne thought. *But this is far too cruel a punishment, and it has gone on for far too long.*

She smiled at Theseus.

"I'll be back soon."

She left and searched the entire palace for Daedalus. When she finally found the man, she told him about her plans and her worries, asking him for any advice she could give Theseus so that he might survive the Labyrinth.

Daedalus thought about the matter. Then he reached for his chest and gave the young princess a ball of silver thread.

"The thread will glimmer in the dark," he said. "Instruct the young Athenian prince to carry it with him. Tell him that with each step he takes, he must unwind the thread. If he and his people survive the Minotaur, then all they'll need to do to is follow the silver thread back to the beginning."

Ariadne thanked Daedalus and immediately returned to Theseus. She gave him the ball of silver thread and Daedalus's instructions.

"I'll be waiting for you by the entrance. And when you get out—"

"When I get out, we'll go to Athens. Together," Theseus said. "Thank you, Ariadne. You have saved us all."

Ariadne giving Theseus the thread.
No restrictions;
https://commons.wikimedia.org/wiki/File:The_golden_fleece_and_the_heroes_who_lived_befor e_Achilles_(1921)_(14786798643).jpg

The night came to an end, and Helios (the god of the sun) rose to start his journey across the blue sky, bringing with him a new day. Theseus and the other Athenians were taken from their cells and shoved inside the Labyrinth.

Luckily, Theseus had managed to keep a sword hidden behind his cape. As soon as the doors to the dark Labyrinth closed behind him and the other tributes, he removed it, along with the silver thread given to him by Ariadne.

The Athenians all closed ranks around their prince, the young boys on the outside, the young girls in the middle. Theseus stayed in the front.

Words cannot describe the horrors of the Minotaur's Labyrinth, but we will try all the same. Its walls were said to be seven times as tall as a man and so smooth that no one could ever hope to climb them. The halls were barely wide enough to fit three men standing shoulder to shoulder, giving its captives little room to fight or evade the monster's savage attacks. Every noise was amplified, the echoes of every breath and every step following you.

Theseus's grip on his sword tightened. He knew no more Athenians could be subjected to this torment.

Just as Ariadne and Daedalus had instructed him, he unwound the silver thread with each step he took. He went farther and farther into the Labyrinth, always vigilant around corners, always ready to attack at a moment's notice.

Along the way, he saw bloodstains and skulls and bones of the tributes that came before. While the sight struck fear in the hearts of the other young tributes, it only served to fuel the fire burning inside Theseus.

Finally, as they were about to reach the center of the Labyrinth—the rumored favorite dwelling place of the monster—the Minotaur came into sight.

"Step back," Theseus whispered to his fellow tributes. "Stay as far back as you can."

They did not need to be told twice. They stepped back as far as they could while still being able to keep an eye on their prince.

Theseus stared down his enemy. The Minotaur was twice as large as a regular man, his bulging muscles and massive hands betraying his immense strength. From toe to neck, he resembled a human, with the single exception of a tail on his rear. Atop his broad shoulders was the hairy head of a bull, with long, thick horns and a wide snout that could smell his prey on the other side of his prison.

The Minotaur's feet started to paw the ground. Theseus readied himself. When the Minotaur charged, he pressed himself against the wall, barely avoiding his enemy's attack. When the Minotaur halted, Theseus did not give him the opportunity to charge again. He ran forward and leaped until he could take the Minotaur by the horns, flinging him to the other side of the Labyrinth.

Theseus did not give the Minotaur a chance to recover. He ran forward and plunged his sword through the monster's heart, slaying it instantly. The Minotaur was no more.

Plate of Theseus slaying the Minotaur. The third figure might be Ariadne.

The Athenians cheered. They congratulated their prince and cried tears of joy. But they were not free yet. Taking the silver thread, they followed it back to the Labyrinth's entrance.

They finally stepped out in the open night air. Just as Ariadne had promised, she was waiting for the Athenians at the entrance. She smiled when she saw Theseus, throwing her arms around him in an embrace.

"Celebrations must come later," Theseus said. "We need to leave before King Minos realizes what we've done."

Taking Ariadne by the hand, Theseus guided her and the other Athenians back to the ship. And so, they sailed away from Crete.

If this was a fairytale, you would now hear about how Prince Theseus married Princess Ariadne, with the two happily ruling over Athens together. But this was no fairytale. Greek heroes are not always chivalrous and good, and even the happiest ending comes with a note of bitterness.

Theseus may have wanted to do right by his people, and his cause may have been just. However, that does not mean he always made the right choices and that he did not hurt people who deserved his respect and loyalty.

Ariadne never made it to Athens. As she slept on the journey there, Theseus and the others abandoned her on the island of Naxos. But you do not need to feel sorry for the Cretan princess. Dionysus, the god of wine, festivity, orchards, and insanity, fell in love with the courageous young girl. He took her as his wife, and Ariadne ascended into godhood, becoming the goddess of thread. Together, they had many children, and Ariadne was happy.

Theseus would live to star in numerous other tales. However, his ending for this one is not so happy. Theseus was so lost in his joyful celebration that he completely forgot the promise he had made his father when he was first entrusted with this quest.

From the moment his son departed Athens, King Aegeus stood on the cliffs, watching the horizon, waiting for those white sails to appear. You can imagine his despair when he saw the Athenian ships in the distance had black sails.

King Aegeus thought his beloved son was dead, killed by the monster that had already taken so many other young souls. The grief was too much. Rather than return to the palace, King Aegeus stepped off the cliff, dying when his body hit the rocks and the water. It was a death made all the more tragic for being so avoidable.

As soon as Theseus stepped onto the shores of Athens, the news came, and the celebrations ended. Theseus was no longer the prince of Athens. Now, he was the king. And yet, he would have given up the crown if it meant having his beloved father with him for just a little while longer.

Activity 2: Multiple Choice

Answer the questions below.

1. Who designed the Labyrinth?
   a) Minos
   b) Daedalus
   c) Ariadne
   d) Poseidon

2. What did Ariadne give Theseus to help him escape?
   a) A sword
   b) A shield
   c) Nothing
   d) Silver thread

3. What are the two main cities of this tale?
   a) Crete and Athens
   b) Sparta and Athens
   c) Argos and Thebes
   d) Thebes and Crete

4. Which deity gave the Cretan Bull to Minos?
   a) Zeus
   b) Dionysius
   c) Poseidon
   d) Aphrodite

5. Who are the parents of the Minotaur?
   a) Aphrodite and Minos
   b) Aphrodite and the Cretan Bull
   c) Poseidon and Pasiphae
   d) Pasiphae and the Cretan Bull

6. How many tributes were sent to the Labyrinth each time?
   a) Fourteen boys
   b) Ten maidens
   c) Ten boys and ten maidens
   d) Seven boys and seven maidens

Chapter 3: Perseus

Perseus's story begins not with a heroic deed but with a fearful king and an act of cruelty.

Acrisius was the king of Argos, and like many kings, he sought the wisdom of the Oracle of Delphi to help rule his city and navigate the Fates' treacherous plans. For years, this helped his city prosper. His hold on the throne remained secured. And yet, despite everything, he only conceived one child, and that child was a daughter.

Worried about his lack of heirs, Acrisius went to the Oracle for help. He asked her when he could expect to finally have a son.

"You? A son?" the Oracle scoffed. "That will never happen. Your daughter, Princess Danae, will have a son, and he will be great. He will be a hero. And one day, you will die by his hand."

Like many men who received terrible prophecies, King Acrisius tried to defy his fate. In doing so, he became cruel and violent. He took his only child, Danae, and locked the young girl inside a bronze room beneath the palace.

For years and years, Danae lived alone in that windowless room. As time passed, she matured into a beautiful young woman. Many learned of the princess's plight, and many tried and failed to rescue her from the prison. No mortal man could do it.

But Danae's famed beauty attracted more than mere mortals. Eventually, word reached Olympus, specifically Zeus, the god of gods. Determined to see Danae for himself, he descended from Olympus in the form of golden rain, the water penetrating into the soil and entering the bronze room.

Zeus found the rumors did Danae little justice and that the princess was far more beautiful than anyone could imagine. He fell in love instantly, and when the golden water made contact with Danae, she became pregnant with Perseus.

Danae and the Shower of Gold

It is said that when King Acrisius heard the baby cry for the first time, he knew it to be the voice of the one who would someday kill him. His next actions are sometimes attributed to mercy and sometimes attributed to self-interest. Some say he did not kill the baby because the cry touched his heart, and he found that he could still spare some love for his infant grandchild. Others say the king knew that those who kill their own family receive the worst punishments in the afterlife. He knew that killing the child would earn him endless torture once he died, so he tried to arrange for the baby's death without being directly responsible for it.

Regardless of what his motive might be, he decided that he could not kill his daughter and grandson. However, he could place them on a raft and send them into the stormy sea.

Luckily for Danae and Perseus, Poseidon, the god of the seas and Zeus's older brother, knew the infant child was his nephew. He calmed the waters and gently guided the raft to the island of Seriphos.

Danae stepped off the raft, holding her infant son. As she wandered the beach, feeling the sand beneath her bare feet, she looked for a safe place for them to rest. That's when she came across a kind fisherman named Dictys. As soon as he heard of Danae's plight, he welcomed them into his home. Soon, he began to view Perseus as if he were his own son and raised the boy as such, guiding him into manhood.

Now, Dictys was not just a regular fisherman. He was the brother of Seriphos's king, Polydectes. At first, Polydectes paid little mind to his brother's new charges. But Danae's beauty eventually charmed him, and he fell madly in love with the former princess. Danae had no interest in marrying anyone, much less the arrogant King Polydectes, as she was focused solely on raising her son.

King Polydectes could not accept such rejection. For years and years, he tried to court Danae, and for years and years, Danae turned him down.

Perseus could see how King Polydectes bothered Danae. Not trusting the man with his mother's heart and honor, he became protective of her, standing between the ill-desired courtship.

Finally, Polydectes could not take it any longer. He decided that it was time to rid himself of the Perseus problem for good. He called both mother and son, welcoming them to his palace with a smile.

"My fair Danae," he said. "I know you have rejected me time and time again. Yet my heart still belongs to you. So how about we come to an agreement?"

"What kind of agreement?" Danae asked.

"It is an agreement that your son must willingly enter as well," Polydectes said. "Should he succeed in bringing me what I ask, I shall give up pursuing your hand and leave you alone for good."

Perseus stepped up. "Name what it is you desire, and you shall have it."

King Polydectes's smile turned cruel.

"I want the head of the mortal Gorgon sister Medusa," Polydectes said. "Bring it to me, and I shall leave your mother alone."

Perseus did not hesitate.

"The head is as good as yours."

And so, Perseus set out on this perilous quest that would finally end his mother's troubles.

You might be familiar with Medusa's name. Perhaps you have even heard a tale or two about how this snake-haired woman came to be. Even back in the times of the ancient Greeks, her story evolved and changed. She went from being a hideous monster to a once-beautiful woman and from a creature filled with unreasonable terror to one whose hatred was rooted in the string of wrongs committed against her.

Originally, the three Gorgon sisters were the daughters of primordial sea deities named Phorcys and Keto. Their names, from oldest to youngest, were Stheno, Euryale, and Medusa. Out of the three, only Medusa was mortal. The Gorgons had scaly skin, large wings, and tusks of a boar, but their snake hair was their most monstrous feature.

With time, the myths around the three sisters changed. They became beautiful, Medusa more so than the other two. She was so beautiful that Poseidon grew to desire her. Some versions of the story portray the union between Poseidon and Medusa as consensual. Others make it very clear that Medusa was raped by the powerful god. Regardless of how the act was committed, both accounts claim that it took place in the temple of Athena.

As you may imagine, the maiden goddess Athena was furious. She felt insulted and disgusted, as she could not believe her temple was desecrated in such a manner. And so, she set out to punish the one person who she could exert her power over. For Poseidon's actions, Medusa was cursed by the goddess of war and wisdom. Her once beautiful hair turned into live snakes, and whoever gazed upon her would be turned to stone.

Statue of Medusa by Gian Lorenzo Bernini.

Perseus would have to slay Medusa to free his mother from Polydectes's torment. While many would consider such actions far more monstrous than anything Medusa did, Perseus was determined to help his mother and prove his worth by any means necessary.

After taking off on his journey, Perseus was visited by Athena and Hermes in his sleep. He received gifts from them that would aid him in his quest.

"I give you, good hero, this mirrored shield, which shall help you in the fight against the Gorgon," Athena said. "And our father, the great god Zeus, sends you this sword."

"I lend to you, good hero, these winged sandals, which shall help in your journey," Hermes said. "And our uncle, the great god Hades of the underworld, sends you this helm of darkness, which shall grant you invisibility. We also give you this sack to carry the Gorgon's head once you have succeeded in your quest."

"Use these gifts wisely, good hero," Athena said. "And begin your journey by seeking out the Gray Sisters. They will be able to tell you where to find the Gorgons."

When Perseus woke up, he found the mirrored shield and great sword in his hands. The winged sandals were on his feet, and by his side were the helm of darkness and the sack to carry the Gorgon's head.

Just as Athena had instructed him, he set out to look for the Gray Sisters. These three witches lived at the edge of the Hyperborean Sea. They were born old, their skins wrinkly and their hairs gray. They were so close to each other that they shared one eye and one tooth between the three of them.

When Perseus found them, he took their eye and held it out of their reach. Distressed, the three witches demanded he return it to them immediately.

"Only if you tell me the way to the Gorgon sisters," Perseus said. "If you do not tell me the truth, not only will I keep your eye, but I shall also take your tooth. Without it, all three of you will starve to death."

"All right, all right!" the three sisters cried. "We will tell you where to find them."

They gave Perseus instructions to fly south, all the way to the end of the world. There, in a land of burning heat, in a cave surrounded by stone statues, he would find the three Gorgon sisters.

"Thank you," Perseus said, returning their eye to them. "I shall leave you in peace."

And so, Perseus followed their instructions. Using the winged sandals gifted to him by Hermes, he flew south until he found the land the Gray Sisters spoke of.

He landed on the ground, arriving at midday. He saw a stone statue, its face contorted in horror as the person let out an eternal, silent scream. Just ahead, he saw two more. He walked toward them, seeing the same fearful expression on their faces. Then he saw three more statues just a few more paces in front of him. He continued to follow this trail until he found the cave.

Perseus took in a long, deep breath. He tried to memorize the lay of the land as best as he could, then he held out his shield so that it would reflect the path he must follow. With small, silent steps, he advanced into the cave.

The Gorgons were asleep. Medusa lay safely in the arms of her two older, immortal sisters.

Seeing this, Perseus hesitated for a second. They looked so peaceful that it seemed wrong to hunt them down as if they were monsters. But then he remembered his mother, and he remembered he gave his word that he would bring back Medusa's head. His mother's hand was at stake, as were his honor and reputation.

Perseus's hold on his sword tightened. He lunged forward, aiming for a quick strike, a painless death. But Medusa and her sisters woke up. Medusa shrieked, her cries so dreadful that they struck Perseus with fear for a moment. Still holding up the shield, Perseus advanced and swung his sword. There was silence. Medusa's head fell from her neck and rolled on the ground until it lay at Perseus's feet. The mortal Gorgon was dead. From her blood, Pegasus, the famed winged stallion, was born.

Perseus defeating Medusa.
https://commons.wikimedia.org/wiki/File:Perseus_med_Medusahuvudet.jpg

Quickly, Perseus put the head inside the sack given to him by the gods. The two other remaining Gorgons, Stheno and Euryale, were furious. One held their fallen sister's body, while the other charged at

Perseus, ready to avenge Medusa.

But Perseus was quick. He put on the helm of darkness, which turned him invisible. He hurried out of the cave and leaped into the air, letting Hermes's sandals carry him away from that cursed land.

Though Perseus had not planned it so, the place he decided to rest for the night just happened to be where Atlas was located. He held up the heavens as punishment for challenging Zeus and the other Olympians during the Titanomachy. Nearby was the garden where Atlas's orchard of golden apples grew from majestic trees. These were tended by the Hesperides, the golden nymphs of the evening and the daughters of the great Titan.

"Greetings, oh great Titan," Perseus said as he approached the godly being. "I am Perseus, son of the god Zeus and the mortal Danae. I have just finished a gruesome quest and require rest for the night."

In ancient Greece, the practice of *xenia* (hospitality) was not just good manners. It was a sacred moral obligation that everyone, god or mortal, was obligated to abide by. If a host refused their guest or if a guest dishonored their host, their actions would be seen as a personal insult and a criminal offense. By all accounts, Atlas should have welcomed Perseus and made him as comfortable as possible for as long as Perseus stayed with him.

But that was not what happened. You see, long ago, Atlas heard a prophecy claiming that a son of Zeus would steal three of his golden apples. The moment Perseus identified himself as such, Atlas feared this was the man the prophecy spoke of and immediately refused to serve Perseus food and wine. He also refused to give him a good place to rest.

Furious and beyond insulted, Perseus turned his head to the side, closing his eyes as he took out Medusa's head from the sack, holding it out in front of Atlas. Immediately, Atlas turned to stone.

Now, the prophecy that Atlas heard was correct. One day, a son of Zeus would come to his garden and steal three golden apples. However, that son was not Perseus but Herakles.

Perseus continued on his journey, and on the way back to Seriphos, he flew by the kingdom of Aethiopia.

In Aethiopia, there lived a king named Cepheus, a queen named Cassiopeia, and a beautiful princess named Andromeda. Their kingdom was rich, their land majestic, and their reign secure. In their comfort and prosperity, the king and queen grew proud. One day, Queen Cassiopeia made a huge mistake.

"My daughter Andromeda is the most beautiful young woman alive," she boasted to all. "Why, I believe she is even more beautiful than the sea nymphs, the Nereids."

Boasting superiority over godly beings, even when true, is always a dangerous thing to do. Cassiopeia's words invoked the wrath of the Nereids and the god of the sea, Poseidon. A giant serpent-like sea monster known as Cetus was sent to the shores of Aethiopia to cause terror as punishment for the queen's careless boast.

King Cepheus and Queen Cassiopeia went to the Oracle for advice on to save their kingdom.

"Cetus was sent because of your boasting about Princess Andromeda's beauty," the Oracle said. "Therefore, the only way to appease Poseidon and the Nereids is to offer the princess as a sacrifice to the sea monster."

King Cepheus and Queen Cassiopeia were distraught. They knew they had a responsibility to their people, but how could they possibly sacrifice their daughter?

Andromeda took the news with solemnity and understanding.

"If that is what must be done to protect our people and our city, then that is what we shall do."

Andromeda was stripped of all her clothing and tied to a rock in the sea, where she would await her fate at the hands of Cetus. From the shores, the people of Aethiopia watched their brave princess offer herself as a sacrifice to save them all. King Cepheus and Queen Cassiopeia already mourned the loss of their beloved daughter.

This scene greeted Perseus as he flew over the Aethiopian Sea on his way back to Seriphos. He halted mid-flight, struck not just by the horror of the situation but also by Andromeda's incredible beauty.

Determined to save the distressed yet courageous maiden, Perseus flew to her side.

"My fair maiden! I'm Perseus, son of Zeus and slayer of the Gorgon!" he greeted. "What is your name, and why do I find you here, naked and defenseless, tied to this rock?"

"I am Princess Andromeda of Aethiopia, daughter of King Cepheus and Queen Cassiopeia," Andromeda said. "As to why I am here, worry not about such things, brave hero. This is not of your concern."

"I beg to differ, my princess," Perseus said. "You are in clear danger. I would not be a hero if I abandoned you."

"I am here out of my own will," Andromeda insisted, still holding her composure even as the waves grew more violent. "I am offering myself as a sacrifice to the monster that has been tormenting my people. If my death can save my beloved Aethiopia, then I'll gladly die for its sake."

Moved by the princess's words, Perseus knew that he could not leave Andromeda to this dark fate.

"You are here to spare your people from suffering. I wager that this sea monster has been causing havoc and pain, has it not?" Perseus asked. "But if there were no sea monster, there would be no need for a sacrifice."

"Indeed, there would not," Andromeda said. "Unfortunately, that is not the reality we live in, son of Zeus."

"Maybe not now. But it will be soon."

Holding out his sword and shield, Perseus stood on top of the rock that Andromeda was tied to. He waited for hours and hours for Cetus to come, the waves around them growing more and more violent, the tell-tale signs of a dangerous storm coming. Neither princess nor hero wavered in their resolution.

Finally, they saw dorsal fins that were larger than temples breaking through the water's surface, swimming toward them. Andromeda took a deep breath but did not let her fear show. Perseus's grip on his sword tightened.

"Worry not," Perseus said to Andromeda. "I will let no harm come to you."

"Perseus said, 'Fair damsel, put all fear aside—I have
freed you—and now you belong to me.'"

Perseus and Andromeda

Perseus flew to meet Cetus. As if it were sensing the approach of the
hero, the serpent-like creature leaped out of the water, letting out a
horrific cry.

However, Perseus was not intimidated. He continued to fly at top
speed. As he was about to make contact with Cetus, he drew his sword
back and then thrust it forward, piercing the monster's scales.

Cetus cried again, this time in pain. With his sword still partially
inside the monster's body, Perseus flew up, creating a long, deep cut.

The battle continued. The people of Aethiopia watched in apprehension. Andromeda could not take her eyes off her savior's figure. Time and time again, Perseus evaded Cetus's sharp teeth only to deliver a blow of his own.

Finally, Perseus flew high up in the sky and then plunged downward, his sword held out in front of him. It penetrated the sea creature's skull, killing it for good.

Perseus flew to Andromeda and untied her from the rocks. He gave her his cloak to wrap around her body and then carried her in his arms to the shores of Aethiopia.

As soon as Perseus and Andromeda landed, King Cepheus and Queen Cassiopeia hugged their daughter, kissing her face and weeping tears of joy.

"It is all thanks to the brave Perseus that I am still alive," Andromeda told them. "But I do not understand. Wasn't my sacrifice required to save our land? Will there be another monster sent our way?"

"No," responded the Oracle. "The offer of you as a sacrifice was required, Princess. Not your actual death. You offered yourself to Cetus, and to save you, the hero slayed the monster."

"So, he helped not just me but also all of us and our city," Andromeda said. She looked at Perseus and smiled. "Thank you, son of Zeus."

"Yes, thank you," said the king. "You are forever a friend of our people. No deed could ever repay you enough for what you did for us, but if there is any favor you need, tell us, and it shall be yours."

"Thank you, Your Majesty," said Perseus. "For now, a good place to rest and good wine to drink should be enough."

"Then you shall be a guest of honor in our palace and sit with us at our table!"

While Perseus stayed in Aethiopia, he and Princess Andromeda fell in love. Seeing this and still grateful to the hero who saved his daughter and his people, King Cepheus approached the two youths and asked them whether they would like to be wed.

Both Perseus and Andromeda eagerly agreed to the proposal, and a lavish wedding was scheduled for the end of the week.

The bride and groom were honored and delighted by the celebrations. King Cepheus and Queen Cassiopeia knew they could not have chosen a better suitor for their daughter. However, in giving Perseus Andromeda's hand in marriage, they greatly offended Phineus, son of Belus and brother of Cepheus.

At nightfall, Phineus barged into the feast uninvited.

"Andromeda was my betrothed!" Phineus declared. "How dare you wed her to someone else, brother!"

King Cepheus stood up.

"When my daughter's life was in danger, you did not come to her aid," the king said. "You do not care for Andromeda's safety or her happiness. You only wanted her because she could help you secure a claim to my throne. I cannot let my beloved daughter marry someone who would treat her in such a way."

But such reasoning did little to appease Phineus's fury. He raised his spear and threw it at his rival. Though Perseus easily evaded the attack, others were not so lucky. A battle unfolded, with Phineus's followers attacking the wedding guests.

Perseus watched blood be spilled at the feast meant to honor his holy union with his beloved. First, he was horrified. But he grew furious. Determined to put an end to this horror, he cried out, "Those who are a friend to me and my wife, close your eyes and turn your head! This is your only warning."

The wedding guests did as Perseus instructed. Perseus closed his own eyes, reached for the sack he always carried with him, and took out Medusa's head.

He held Medusa's severed head as high as possible. As soon as he heard the sounds of blades cease, he placed the head back in the sack and opened his eyes. All around him, his enemies, apart from Phineus, had turned to stone. His wedding guests who had wisely closed their eyes and looked away were still there.

Sebastian Ricci's painting of Perseus showing Phineus the head of Medusa.
https://commons.wikimedia.org/wiki/File:Sebastiano_Ricci_-
Perseus_Confronting_Phineus_with_the_Head_of_Medusa_-_86.PA.591_-_J._Paul_Getty_Museum.jpg

"You may open your eyes now, my friends. It is safe."

One by one, the guests opened their eyes and marveled at the scene surrounding them. Dozens, if not hundreds, of armed men were frozen in place, the horror forever carved in their features.

But they were not the only ones amazed by this sight. Realizing Perseus's might, Phineus fell to his knees, begging the hero for mercy.

Perseus walked toward him slowly.

"You came here on my wedding day and attacked my friends and my family," Perseus said. "You insulted my marriage during a time of celebration. You put all of these good people at risk because of your pride and because you wanted a claim to Aethiopia's throne. And yet you dare ask me for mercy?"

Perseus reached inside the sack. This time, the guests did not need to be told to close their eyes and look away.

"You are a coward," Perseus said and held out the Gorgon's head in front of Phineus's face, freezing him forever in that position. "You deserve no mercy."

Perseus and Andromeda stayed in Aethiopia for a while longer before Perseus announced he had to return to Seriphos. As his wife, Andromeda was to accompany him. They bid King Cepheus and Queen Cassiopeia farewell before embarking on their journey.

When Perseus arrived on the island, he did not see anyone. He learned that Dictys's wife had passed away while Perseus was on his quest, and Polydectes continued his loathsome, dishonorable pursuit of Danae's hand in marriage. The king had been so insistent and so repugnant that Dictys and Danae fled the main city and sought refuge at a temple.

"This cannot go on any longer," Perseus said to himself. "Polydectes has tormented my mother for far too long, and his disgraceful character has brought nothing but misery to the people of Seriphos. He is a tyrant and a villain, and I have let him get away with his cruelty for far too long."

He soon learned that Polydectes was holding a feast for those who supported his rule anger. And at the palace, Perseus found his enemy. As he marched into the main hall, Perseus could hear their merrymaking, their laughter echoing all around him as they feasted and drank enough wine to serve the entire city. The sounds only further incentivized Perseus.

As soon as he stepped into the hall, all eyes, including those of Polydectes, turned to him. Perseus was a commanding figure even under ordinary circumstances, but given that none of the men of Seriphos expected him to survive the quest for the Gorgon's head, the sight was especially surprising.

Perseus barely held back a smirk. He reached for his sack, closed his eyes, and looked away. He held Medusa's head high, and just as had happened on his wedding feast, all sound stopped. He put the head back and opened his eyes. Just as he had planned, the palace's dining hall was now filled with statues, including Polydectes.

"Now my mother and the people of Seriphos are free of your tyranny forever, Polydectes."

Perseus returned to Andromeda, who, under Perseus's instructions, was hiding in his childhood home. They showed the people of Seriphos that Polydectes could harm them no more, and in exchange, they told Perseus where he could find his mother and his father figure. Perseus and Andromeda went to the temple where they were hiding, and as soon as she saw her son, Danae brought him into her arms with a warm embrace.

"Oh, my dear son!" she cried. "I knew you would come back to us!"

Perseus hugged his mother tightly.

"I am back, Mother. I am sorry it took me this long."

Perseus then introduced his mother and wife, and the two women got along almost immediately. As they talked and got to know one another, Perseus turned to Dictys.

"I am sorry to hear about your wife."

"Thank you," Dictys said. "We grieved her greatly. I will not lie; it was difficult to deal with Polydectes while you were gone. But now that you are back, I hope things will be a little easier."

"Yes, they will, but not for the reason you might think."

Perseus then told Dictys and his mother all about his journey, about slaying the Gorgon, facing Atlas, saving Andromeda, their wedding feast, and what he had done to Polydectes.

"His days of tyranny are over," Perseus said to Dictys. He then turned to his mother. "He cannot torment you anymore, Mother."

Crying tears of joy, Danae once more embraced her son, kissing his head and smiling, unburdened for the first time in years.

"But now that Polydectes is gone, Seriphos needs a new king," Perseus declared. Though his arms were still around his mother, he addressed Dictys. "You were always good to us. When we arrived on these shores, you gave us food and shelter. You made us family. You are kind and wise, and the people of Seriphos know you care for them. You were Polydectes's brother. You have a claim to the crown, Dictys, and I cannot think of anyone better for the job."

Though Dictys was hesitant at first, the humble man eventually accepted the responsibilities of kingship. He offered Danae, Perseus, and Andromeda a more lavish home close to the palace, but the three turned down the offer.

"My son and I came to Seriphos from Argos due to my father's cruelty," Danae said. "Years and years have passed since then; I wish to know if time has tempered my father's superstitious mind."

The three set out for Argos, ready to meet Acrisius. Though Danae hoped for the best, Perseus was ready to defend his mother and wife should the need arise. However, when they arrived in Argos, they were shocked to find that Acrisius was no longer there. He heard word of his daughter and grandson's return. Still fearful of the prophecy, he went into voluntary exile.

When Danae heard the news, she was crestfallen.

"Perhaps reconciliation between us is truly impossible," she lamented.

Perseus put a hand on Danae's shoulder.

"Do not despair, Mother," he said. "I know you wanted to understand why your father caused you so much suffering, and I know you hoped to make amends. But perhaps this is for the best. Regardless of what my grandfather may do or think, you will always have Andromeda and I by your side."

"Indeed," Andromeda said. "We are family now, and we are honored to stay by your side for as long as you need."

Time passed, and the three settled in Argos, living happily together. Eventually, there came word that the new king of Larissa was holding funeral games in honor of his recently deceased father. These were athletic competitions in which men from all over Greece were invited to show their prowess.

Eager to participate, Perseus, Danae, and Andromeda traveled to the large city, and Perseus signed up for the discus-throwing competition.

Perseus held the disc. He spun around the circle, gaining momentum before releasing it. The disc flew high, traveling far, and when it landed, it hit a spectator in the head, killing him instantly.

That spectator, as you might have already guessed, was King Acrisius. While trying to run away from his grandson and avoid his fate, he took refuge in the city. And so it was that the prophecy was fulfilled.

Perseus did not become the king of Argos, feeling that to be dishonorable. However, he did eventually establish the great stronghold of Mycenae. He and Andromeda had nine children together, one of whom was Electryon. Electryon would eventually have a daughter named Alcmene, and Alcmene would someday have a son by Zeus who would be known as Herakles.

As for Medusa's head, Perseus eventually gifted the head to Athena, who used it to create Zeus's famed shield, the aegis.

Activity 3: Open-close Exercise

In each sentence, circle the correct answer.

1. Perseus was the son of *Zeus/Poseidon* and the mortal princess Danae.

2. When Danae and Perseus arrived at Seriphos, *Polydectes/Dictys* welcomed them into his home.

3. Medusa was cursed by *Poseidon/Athena* to have snake hair that would turn whoever looked at her into stone.

4. To aid him in his quest, Athena and *Hermes/Aphrodite* and Zeus gave Perseus poison arrows, a club, and a *golden thread/a mirrored shield*, winged sandals, and the helm of darkness.

5. Andromeda, daughter of *Cepheus/Phineus* and Cassiopeia, was the princess of *Argos/Aethiopia*.

6. After defeating Polydectes, Perseus, Andromeda, and Danae left Seriphos for *Argos/Larissa*.

Chapter 4: The Twelve Labors of Herakles

In the time of the ancient Greeks, few heroes were more prolific, more revered, and more famous than the mighty Herakles (also spelled as Hercules in the Roman tradition). The stories of his deeds and adventures are far too numerous to recount in one chapter alone. It is difficult to pick a single tale to tell, but we will recount his most famous accomplishment. This is a story not of heroics but of penance and perseverance. It is a story of redemption. It begins with a great tragedy and ends with a great victory. This is the story of the Twelve Labors of Herakles.

To understand why Herakles willingly spent twelve years submitting himself to his cowardly cousin's cruelty, one must first understand how and why Herakles found himself in this predicament.

Herakles was the son of Zeus, but his mother was not Hera, Zeus's wife. His mother was a mortal woman named Alcmene. Zeus admired Alcmene from afar for a long time, despite the fact that Alcmene was married to Amphitryon.

And yet, Zeus still coveted Alcmene. When Amphitryon went to war, Zeus saw an opportunity to finally be with the woman he longed for. Time passed, and just as word came that Amphitryon would soon return from the war, Zeus disguised himself as Amphitryon to trick poor Alcmene into sleeping with him.

It is said that Zeus asked Helios, the godly personification of the sun, not to rise again for three of Earth's rotations so he could spend more time in Alcmene's bed. For three dark days, Zeus kept Alcmene company, his disguise never faltering. The poor woman never realized she was a victim of the god's lustful tricks. And so it was that Herakles was conceived.

The same night Zeus left, Amphitryon returned. He spent the night in his loving wife's bed, and so it was that Herakles's younger twin half-brother, Iphicles, was conceived.

Now, Hera was said to be a vengeful, petty goddess at even the best of times. She was proud and mighty. And she would not stand for any insult. She was not only Zeus's wife but also the goddess of marriage. Her husband's constant infidelity had long tortured her mind and heart. Hera hated Herakles since he was physical proof of Zeus's wandering eyes and restless hands. As long as Herakles lived, Hera could not turn a blind eye to her husband's infidelity.

Herakles grew to be a mighty hero, a strong man whom everyone admired. He married a Theban princess named Megara, daughter of Creon. Together, they had three sons, and Herakles was happy.

Hera could not stand that happiness, not when she was miserable. She hated being reminded of the humiliation she suffered due to Zeus's infidelity. Hera was determined to make Herakles as unhappy as she was, so she used her godly powers to make him temporarily mad.

In his fit of insanity, Herakles slaughtered Megara and their young sons. The poor woman and children were no match for Zeus's son. Not even their anguished cries could snap Herakles out of his madness.

As the sun rose and Hera's madness finally lifted, Herakles found himself surrounded by the bodies of his beloved family. He fell to his knees and cried. Grief paralyzed him as he remembered every horrific second of that terrible night.

Though we would not consider Herakles responsible for his crime today, that was not the case during those times. Perhaps it would not have mattered anyway. Knowing he would have never hurt his family were it not for Hera's doing would have done little to alleviate his guilt and erase those horrible memories. Knowing he was a victim of the gods' cruel whims would not bring back his family.

Herakles searched for a way to purify his soul and make up for the cruelty and pain his horrible strength had unleashed. He found himself at the mercy of his cousin, King Eurystheus of Argos. The king tasked him with ten impossible labors. If Herakles could complete those ten impossible labors, then forgiveness could be granted to him.

Herakles's first labor is known as the Nemean Lion.

"Kill the beast that is terrorizing the village by the mountains," King Eurystheus demanded. "And bring its skin back to me."

The Nemean Lion was invulnerable to weapons, making it impossible to kill it. Yet, Herakles grabbed his club, bronze sword, and arrows.

Herakles tracked the lion to its dwelling, a cave by the mountains. After closing one of the cave's entrances, Herakles cornered the beast so that its only escape route was through him. Herakles drew his bow and fired his arrows, but they bounced off the lion's skin. Then he charged at it with his club, hitting it in the head, momentarily stunning him.

Seeing his opening, Herakles tossed his weapons aside and beat the lion to death with his bare hands. But even though the Nemean Lion had perished, Herakles's task was not complete, for he had to bring its skin back to Eurystheus. He tried to use his sword and his knives, but it was no use.

Hercules and the Nemean Lion.
Metropolitan Museum of Art, CC0, via Wikimedia Commons;
https://commons.wikimedia.org/wiki/File:Hercules_and_the_Nemean_Lion_MET_DT8927.jpg

That was when Athena, the goddess of war and wisdom, appeared before him. She instructed Herakles to use the Nemean Lion's own claws to skin it. Herakles did as instructed, and it worked. He carried the skin all the way back to Argos.

Now, King Eurystheus was not expecting his cousin to survive this task, much less to return to his city. When he was presented with the Nemean Lion's skin, fear struck his heart, as he was faced with the true might of Herakles. He ordered walls to be constructed around Argos and forbade Herakles to ever set foot in the city. From that moment on, he was to wait at the city's gates, and the king would greet him to give him his next task.

Herakles's second labor was to defeat the Lernaean Hydra.

"Defeat the Hydra that lives in the swamps of Lerna," King Eurystheus said. "That shall be your second labor."

And so, Herakles set out to the swamps of Lerna to fight the Lernaean Hydra. He took Iolaus, the son of Herakles's brother, Iphicles. Iolaus was Herakles's nephew and his most beloved companion.

The Hydra was a powerful monster created by Hera. It was a serpentine-like creature that breathed poisonous fumes. The Hydra had multiple heads, and one of them was immortal.

First, Herakles and Iolaus drew the Hydra out into the open with Herakles's flaming arrows. Once the monster was away from the swamps and the lake, Herakles drew out his sword and charged forward, cutting the Hydra's heads one by one. Victory seemed within his grasp, yet he soon learned the terrible secret that made the Hydra such an impossible monster to kill: when one of its non-immortal heads was cut off, two grew in its place.

Hercules and the Lernaean Hydra
National Gallery of Art, CC0, via Wikimedia Commons
https://commons.wikimedia.org/wiki/File:Battista_Angolo_del_Moro,_Hercules_and_the_Hydra,_1552,_NGA_79163.jpg

The heads multiplied and multiplied until Herakles found himself facing a foe that was far stronger than when the battle first started.

Taking advantage of Herakles's horror and confusion, the Hydra charged forward. It wrapped itself around his body, crushing it. Herakles was near death and would perhaps have perished if not for Iolaus's quick thinking.

After distracting the Hydra with fire, Iolaus helped Herakles free himself, and the two scrambled away from the monster.

"What shall we do?" Herakles asked. "How can we defeat such a monster?"

"I think I have an idea," Iolaus said and told Herakles of his plan.

"I think that might work," Herakles said. "That might be the only way we can defeat the Hydra."

Herakles grabbed his sword while Iolaus grabbed a torch. As Herakles cut one of the Hydra's heads, young Iolaus quickly scorched the wound so that it would cauterize, closing it and forming a stump from which no other heads could grow.

They did this to every single one of the Hydra's heads, working together to defeat the monster. When there was only one head left—the middle one, the immortal one—Herakles used the bronze shield that the goddess Athena had given him to cut it off. He hid the head, which was still alive and moving, beneath a giant rock. And just before he and Iolaus returned to Argos, Herakles dipped all his arrows in the Hydra's poisonous blood, crafting a weapon more deadly than even the sharpest of swords.

However, when they arrived at Argos, it was not to celebrations.

"You did not defeat the Hydra on your own, Herakles. Had Iolaus not been there, you would have failed," King Eurystheus said. "Therefore, this task does not count. You still have nine labors to complete."

For Herakles's third, or rather second, labor, he was tasked with capturing the Ceryneian Hind.

"She is a doe that is precious to the maiden goddess Artemis," King Eurystheus said. "I want you to bring her to me."

Herakles readily agreed.

The Ceryneian Hind was no mere doe. Not only was this animal sacred and beloved by the goddess Artemis, but she was also beautiful, with bronze hooves and golden horns. She was said to run faster than the wind.

Herakles knew he could not injure the beautiful animal without enticing Artemis's wrath. And so, he chased the Ceryneian Hind, trying to find a way to bring her back to Argos without causing her harm. He ran after her for a year. Though Herakles would often grow tired, the Ceryneian Hind never once noticed his presence.

Finally, the Ceryneian Hind came to a lake and stopped to drink some water. Seeing his opportunity, Herakles drew his bow and shot an arrow right between her legs. Startled, she jumped back, tripped, and fell. Herakles charged forward and tied her legs, capturing her.

That was when Artemis appeared before him. Herakles humbly explained his predicament to the goddess, who listened quietly.

"Fine," she said. "You may take her to Argos as long as she stays unharmed. After your task is complete, let her return to me."

Thanking the goddess for her generosity, Herakles returned to Argos, taking the Ceryneian Hind with him. Since he was forbidden to enter the city, King Eurystheus had to come out to take the doe from him. The king did so. Just as he stretched out his hand to touch the sacred animal, Herakles smirked and released her from his binds. The Ceryneian Hind, now free, ran back to her mistress.

"It looks like my third labor is complete," Herakles said.

King Eurystheus begrudgingly agreed.

For Herakles's fourth labor, King Eurystheus demanded he capture the Erymanthian Boar.

"The beast lives on Mount Erymanthos," King Eurystheus said. "It is a large, fearsome creature, and you must bring it all the way back to Argos alive."

Herakles set forth to Mount Erymanthos. On his way there, he stopped by to see a friend, the centaur Pholus. Bound by the moral codes of *xenia*, the centaur welcomed his friend and showed him the utmost hospitality. They shared a meal together, and then it was time to share some wine.

Pholus found the only wine he had to serve his friend was one that the god Dionysus had entrusted to the centaurs. He did not think it was a good idea to share it, but he was bound by duty to honor his guest and friend. So, he opened the bottle and served it to Herakles.

As soon as the bottle was opened, centaurs from all over were able to smell its scent. Furious that Pholus was sharing their sacred wine with a human and driven mad by its intoxicating power, they attacked Pholus and Herakles.

Herakles sprang to his feet. He grabbed his arrows, which were still coated with the poisonous Hydra blood, and fired them at the centaurs. As soon as the arrow tips touched their skin, the centaurs fell to the ground, dead. It was a devastating sight.

Pholus was confused as to why so many of his kin had died so quickly. He grabbed one of the arrows to examine it before Herakles could stop him. It slipped from his hand, nicking his skin. Pholus fell dead.

Distraught by the loss of his friend, Herakles was not sure what to do. He went to visit his old tutor, the centaur Chiron, who offered him comfort and advice as to how he could complete his fourth labor.

Herakles thanked Chiron for his help and continued his journey. By this point, winter had fallen in the land, and the mountains of Greece were covered in snow.

Just as Chiron instructed, Herakles drew the Erymanthian Boar out from its hiding place. Once out in the open, Herakles scared the boar away so that it would run and fall into his trap. The Erymanthian Boar ran until it got caught in some thick snow and could no longer continue running. That's when Herakles charged, wrestling the animal and tying its legs together. He threw the boar over his shoulder and returned to Argos, successfully completing his fourth task.

Hercules and the Erymanthian Boar *by Giambologna.*
Giambologna, CC0, via Wikimedia Commons;
https://commons.wikimedia.org/wiki/File:Hercules_and_the_Erymanthian_Boar_MET_DP-927-001.jpg

Herakles's fifth labor is known as the Augean Stables.

"You must go to King Augeas of Alis and clean his stables, where his famed, immortal cattle are kept," King Eurystheus said. "Only once it is completely clean may you consider this task complete."

Herakles readily agreed.

The mighty hero journeyed all the way to Alis and requested an audience with King Augeas.

"Your Majesty, I know your stables need cleaning," Herakles said. "I offer to do the task for you. My only request is that, as payment, you give me one-tenth of your cattle should I manage to accomplish it in one day."

King Augeas looked at Herakles, amused. He knew that such a task was impossible, for he had over a thousand immortal cattle. The stables, vast and impressive as they were, had not been cleaned for over thirty years. King Augeas was familiar with Herakles's fame, but he believed that not even a hero such as he would be able to clean that much muck and dung all by himself, much less in one day.

"Very well," King Augeas agreed. "If you manage to clean the stables by sundown, you shall have my gratitude and one-tenth of my cattle as payment."

Herakles thanked King Augeas and left the palace. Rather than going straight to the stables, he went to the River Alpheus and then to the River Peneus. With his godly strength, he lifted boulders and dug trenches. In doing so, he redirected both rivers so their water would pass through the stables and wash away all the muck and dung, leaving it perfectly clean long before the sunset.

King Augeas was shocked. Herakles was never meant to succeed in completing such an impossible task! Herakles yet again made the impossible possible.

When Herakles went to collect his payment, King Augeas refused to give him any of his cattle.

"Why should I pay you when the only reason you even offered to clean my stables was that King Eurystheus of Argos ordered you to do so?" King Augeas asked. "This is a matter between the both of you. You should have never demanded payment for a task you were honor bound to complete."

"You speak of my honor, yet you refuse to honor your own word," Herakles said. "You said if the stables were clean by sundown, I could have one-tenth of your cattle *and* your gratitude. The stables are clean, and the sun is still in the sky. Yet you refuse to give me both."

Both men refused to budge, so King Augeas's son, Prince Phyleus, stepped in to try to resolve the matter. He listened to both men's cases.

He had witnessed his father agree to Herakles's terms, and he had also witnessed Herakles complete the task as asked. Though King Augeas was his father, Phyleus sided with Herakles, claiming his father was honor bound to keep his word.

Angry and betrayed, King Augeas refused. He banished Herakles from his city and sent Prince Phyleus into exile. However, Herakles could not stand for such an injustice to be committed toward someone who spoke the truth.

"I promise, my friend, that I will not rest until this wrong is righted," Herakles said.

And so, Herakles fought by Phyleus's side to undo the injustice. He killed King Augeas and helped Phyleus take the throne. Only then did he return to Argos.

Once he arrived at the gates, he found that word of his deeds had reached the city before him. King Eurystheus greeted him with smugness.

"You did not clean the stables, Herakles. The rivers did it for you," King Eurystheus said. "Therefore, this task does not count. You still have six other labors to complete."

Herakles's sixth labor centered around the Stymphalian Birds.

"The Stymphalian Birds have made the swamp areas around Lake Stymphalia their home," King Eurystheus said. "They have eaten the crops and terrorized the townspeople. Rid the people of this menace!"

The Stymphalian Birds were no ordinary birds. They were sacred to the god Ares, the god of war. Their beaks were made of bronze, and their feathers were as sharp as swords. They were said to be carnivorous, feasting on the flesh of men, and their excrement was toxic to most living things. The birds reproduced rapidly and thrived around the swamp areas of Lake Stymphalia. The people who lived nearby suffered, as they were unable to take on the large flock.

When Herakles arrived at the location, he found himself facing a difficult obstacle. Herakles was strong and mighty, but his weight was too great to traverse the swamps. He could not face the birds in close combat, so he needed to find another way to free the townsfolk of their troubles.

That was when Athena came to his aid once more. She gave him a rattle that had been crafted by the god Hephaestus, the god of blacksmiths and artisans. She instructed him to use the rattle to create a noise that would scare away the birds. When they flew up into the sky, he could use his poisonous arrows to shoot them.

Herakles did as he was instructed. As soon as he shook the rattle, a great, terrible noise filled the air. The entire flock immediately flew toward the heavens. Determined to ensure they would never return to the area, Herakles took out his bow and shot as many of the birds as he could. He did not get all of them, but those who did escape his arrows never returned to Lake Stymphalia. And so his sixth labor was complete.

Pottery with a scene of Herakles attacking the Stymphalian Birds.
https://commons.wikimedia.org/wiki/File:Herakles_Stymphalian_BM_B163.jpg

Herakles's seventh labor involved the infamous Cretan Bull.

We talked about this creature before, but if you forgot, do not worry. King Minos of Crete prayed to the god Poseidon, king of the seas and of storms, to help him prove to the world his right to rule. In answer to his prayer, Poseidon sent him a mighty white bull—the Cretan Bull—with the explicit orders that when the time came, the bull would be sacrificed to Poseidon.

However, King Minos saw how people marveled at the animal. He thought the bull was far too great to be sacrificed like common cattle. He tried to trick the god by sacrificing a different bull instead.

But tricking the gods is never a wise idea. When Poseidon found out about this, he was angry and insulted. He asked the goddess Aphrodite, the goddess of love and beauty, to put a curse on King Minos's wife, Pasiphae, so that she would fall in love with the Cretan Bull. From that cursed union, Pasiphae gave birth to the infamous half-man, half-bull creature known as the Minotaur.

"Bring me the Cretan Bull, the father of the Minotaur," King Eurystheus said. "And bring him to me *alive.*"

And so, Herakles sailed to Crete.

When he arrived, King Minos welcomed him with a feast. The two men talked over wine, and Herakles explained his predicament.

"You may have the beast if you can catch him," King Minos said. "But be warned that he is no ordinary bull. He was created by a god. Ever since the birth of his monstrous child, he has been causing chaos all over my city, destroying our crops and terrorizing my people. If you can catch him and take him away from here, I would be eternally grateful."

Herakles thanked King Minos for his understanding and promised he would do his best to help Crete. When Minos offered to give him any assistance he might need, Herakles politely refused.

"It is generous of you to offer, Your Majesty, but this is a task I must complete alone."

"Well, until you do, you are an honored guest in my city."

Herakles observed the beast for days, stalking it and learning its strengths. Finally, when he was ready, he snuck behind the bull. When the animal least expected it, Herakles wrestled it to the ground. With his strong arms wrapped around its neck, he tamed the creature until it was almost dead. Then he hauled it to his ship and sailed back to Argos.

Hercules and the Cretan Bull *by Giambologna.*
Giambologna, CC0, via Wikimedia Commons;
https://commons.wikimedia.org/wiki/File:Hercules_and_the_Cretan_Bull_MET_91174.jpg

When King Eurystheus saw that Herakles had succeeded in completing yet another impossible task, he was furious. He thought about sacrificing the Cretan Bull to Hera, who was known to hate Herakles, as a way to insult the hero. Hera scoffed at the idea. She would not accept a sacrifice that could, in some way, be interpreted as exonerating Herakles and his actions.

So, the Cretan Bull was set loose. Eventually, he made his way to Marathon, where he would become known as the Marathonian Bull. It would not be until years later that Theseus, the slayer of the Minotaur, would capture the bull and finally sacrifice him to the gods.

For Herakles's eighth labor, he was to steal the Mares of Diomedes.

"Those mares are said to be unlike any in this world," King Eurystheus said. "And I want them for myself."

King Eurystheus thought this would certainly be the task that stopped Herakles's heroics. Diomedes was the king of Thrace, and his cruelty was well known. His mares were beautiful and strong, but they were not given the plants and vegetables they craved. Instead, the poor creatures were fed human flesh. This corrupt, terrible diet drove them to madness, making them impossible to tame.

Knowing King Diomedes would not welcome Herakles to Thrace the way Minos had, the hero brought along a group of volunteers. Among them was one of his dearest and most beloved friends, a youth by the name of Abderos.

Sure enough, Herakles's fears were proven right. Rather than welcoming them, King Diomedes sent his own men to face Herakles and his volunteers in battle. Determined not to fail, Herakles went to face Diomedes himself to demand he stop the madness.

Unfortunately, during the time he was gone, his favorite companion, Abderos, was killed by one of Diomedes's men.

Struck by grief, Herakles decided to avenge his dear Abderos. He ran his bronze sword through Diomedes, killing him on the spot. Then he fed the cruel king to his mad mares.

Whatever curse had plagued the mares was lifted as soon as they tasted the flesh of their tormentor. They became as tame and tranquil as regular horses. Taking advantage of their new subdued demeanor, Herakles tied their mouths and brought them to Argos.

As soon as King Eurystheus saw the infamous mares, fear filled him. He wished to sacrifice them to Hera, but the goddess believed them impure due to the diet forced upon them. So, the mares were set loose to roam Greece until the day they roamed too close to Mount Olympus, and Zeus had them murdered by other wild animals.

Herakles's ninth labor was to bring King Eurystheus the Belt of Hippolyta.

"The queen of the Amazons is a daughter of Ares. She is a fierce warrior, and her leather belt, which she uses to carry her weapons, is said to grant its wearer special powers," King Eurystheus said. "My daughter, Princess Admete, covets that belt, and so you must bring it to me."

Herakles agreed, thinking that this task would be easy to accomplish. Queen Hippolyta was a fierce warrior and a just ruler. Surely, she would not have a problem parting with her belt when she heard of Herakles's plight.

Just as Herakles expected, Hippolyta welcomed Herakles and his men. When she heard of his predicament, she readily agreed to give him her belt. However, Hera could not stand the idea of Herakles accomplishing yet another task, and she decided to interfere.

She convinced the other Amazons that Herakles and his men were invaders who intended to kill their beloved queen. The Amazons grabbed their weapons and charged Herakles and his men, ready to defend Hippolyta.

A bloody battle broke out. Herakles's men were strong, but so were the Amazons. They were famed for having invented the art of fighting on horseback. No matter what Herakles tried, he could not gain control of the situation. Soon, he was forced to draw his blade to defend his men. Queen Hippolyta found herself in the same situation, though they were on opposite sides.

The battle continued, with men and women falling. It was only when Herakles killed Queen Hippolyta and retrieved the belt that the chaos finally came to an end. As the Amazons mourned their beloved queen, Herakles returned to Argos and gave King Eurystheus and his daughter the famed leather belt.

For Herakles's tenth labor, Eurystheus demanded he bring the Cattle of Geryon to him.

"Geryon is a monstrous warrior with three heads and three sets of limbs. He lives in Erythia in the far, far west," King Eurystheus said. "I want you to bring me his cattle."

The travel to Erythia was long and perilous. To get there, Herakles was forced to traverse the Libyan Desert. For days, he endured the intense and unforgiving heat with no complaint. But even the mighty Herakles could grow angry when exhausted and thirsty. He let out his frustration by firing an arrow at the sun.

Luckily for Herakles, the god Helios was not offended by his action. Instead, the god was impressed and amused by his strength. He decided to help Herakles on his journey. He gave him a golden cup with which Herakles could sail the sea every night.

Following the god's instructions, Herakles finally arrived in Erythia. When his foot touched the shores, Geryon's two-headed Orthus, who was the guardian of the cattle, charged at Herakles.

Herakles grabbed his club. Before either of the dog's heads could take a bite out of him, he swung the club, killing the animal instantly.

However, Herakles's trial was not done. Next came Eurytion, the herdsman who cared for Geryon's cattle. Herakles killed the man just as he had killed the dog.

Next came Geryon himself. Though Herakles had heard of his might, stature, and power, the tales did not prepare him for the sight of the monstrous warrior. Geryon was furious at Herakles, and he charged forward, ready for battle.

Herakles jumped out of the way. Seeing that he would not be able to defeat his new enemy with his club, he instead grabbed his bow and a poison arrow, shooting it at Geryon. As soon as the tip made contact with Geryon's skin, the monstrous warrior fell dead on the ground.

"Finally," Herakles said. "Now, to bring the cattle back with me to Argos."

Unfortunately for Herakles, Hera's hatred for Herakles was strong. She scared the cattle, causing them to scatter and run all over Greece.

Hercules and Geryon's Cattle.
Rijksmuseum, CC0, via Wikimedia Commons;
https://commons.wikimedia.org/wiki/File:Hercules_hoedt_de_kudde_van_Geryon_Augiae_stab ulum_egerit_(titel_op_object)_Herculische_thema%27s_(serietitel),_RP-P-OB-52.353.jpg

A year passed as Herakles tried to get all of them back. It was hard, exhausting, and frustrating work, but Herakles managed to do it all the same. Still, Hera could not let things go. As Herakles and the cattle journeyed back to Argos, she flooded a river so the cattle would not be able to cross it.

But the goddess underestimated Herakles's determination and wit. He gathered rocks and boulders and threw them into the river. He did this for hours and hours until the stones created a path the cattle could use to cross.

"Here are the cattle," Herakles said, "All of them are here, just as you asked."

King Eurystheus took the cattle and immediately ordered them to be sacrificed to the goddess Hera.

This should have been the end of Herakles's plight. But if you remember, King Eurystheus refused to count the slaying of the Lernaean Hydra and the cleaning of the Augean Stables. Thus, Herakles had two more labors to complete before his penance was done.

Herakles's eleventh labor—or ninth, if you were to ask King Eurystheus—centered around the Golden Apples of Hesperides.

"Bring me three of those golden apples," King Eurystheus said. "And then your task will be complete."

The Hesperides were nymphs, said to be daughters of the Titan Atlas. These beautiful beings always appeared in three. They lived in a magnificent garden in the far, far west. They were also said to be the daughters of the evening, the nymphs of sunsets, and they were said to be as beautiful as the golden light that bathes the sky just as day is about to end. Herakles would find the tree with the three golden apples King Eurystheus desired somewhere deep in their garden.

The Garden of the Hesperides by Frederic Leighton.
https://commons.wikimedia.org/wiki/File:Frederic_Leighton_-_The_Garden_of_the_Hesperides.jpg

Herakles set out on his journey. On the way there, he met the Titan Prometheus, who had long ago defied the gods by stealing the fire of knowledge and gifting it to humanity. To punish him, Zeus tied him to a boulder. Every day, he endured the torture of having Zeus's eagle eat his regenerating liver.

Taking pity on the fire thief and creator of humanity, Herakles drew his bow and killed the eagle. Prometheus and Herakles both knew this was just a temporary relief from the endless torment inflicted on the Titan. But when one had already suffered for years and years and was destined to suffer for years and years to come, any small amount of respite was a godly mercy.

As they talked, Herakles told Prometheus of his quest. Prometheus nodded sagely.

"I should not tell you this, but since you have helped me, I feel bound to help you in return," Prometheus said. "Only Atlas can retrieve the golden apple from the tree in the Hesperides' garden. If you must bring King Eurystheus three of them, then you must find a way to get Atlas to pick the apples for you."

Herakles thanked Prometheus for his advice, and he set out back on his journey.

However, finding the garden was harder than Herakles originally thought. He knew it to be in the west, yet it was well hidden. And so, he went after the Old Man of the Sea, a shape-shifting water creature who would answer any question asked of him as long as one was able to hold him down as he changed forms.

It didn't take long for Herakles to find the Old Man of the Sea. Herakles was able to wrestle him down with his mighty strength. The creature shifted between various different beings, yet Herakles still held on, pinning him to the ground, his arms tightly wrapped around his neck.

Finally, after what seemed like an eternity, the creature gave in and told Herakles where to find the garden and Atlas.

When Herakles finally reached the Titan who carried the heavens on his shoulder, he told him of his predicament and his quest to bring King Eurystheus three golden apples from his daughters' garden.

"I understand you must complete this impossible task to cleanse your soul from that unspeakable sin, and I understand why you are so determined to see it done," Atlas said. "But as you can see, I have my own burden to shoulder. I cannot leave my post."

Herakles considered the situation. "I am a son of Zeus. As such, though I am mortal, I have his godly strength," Herakles said. "I'll carry the heavens on my shoulders while you go to the garden and pick the three golden apples for me."

Atlas regarded Herakles suspiciously.

"Are you sure you can do this?"

"I am the mighty Herakles. I've done ten impossible labors so far. I can carry your burden as well."

And so, Atlas gave Herakles the heavens. As soon as he felt that immense weight on his shoulders, Herakles's knees buckled. He grunted and groaned, and his arms and his legs shook. His back and his neck hurt as he exerted himself more than ever before to hold up the sky. Atlas waited for a moment with bated breath. Though Herakles struggled, he did not let the heavens fall.

"You truly do have the strength of Zeus, mighty mortal," Atlas said in awe. "Very well. I shall go pick the three apples you requested."

Atlas did as he said, going to his daughters' garden and picking the three golden apples with ease. When Herakles saw him approaching, he smiled, relieved.

"You've returned! Now come, carry your burden once more so I can finish my quest."

But Atlas shook his head. Though he had only been free from his punishment for a little while, he could not stand the idea of going back to carrying the heavens. Now that Herakles had proved he could do so, he saw no reason why he should not enjoy his freedom.

"I have endured that punishment for more time than you can even imagine," Atlas said. "I will not submit myself to it again."

"Very well. I endured not even a fraction of what you did, and I already feel tired," Herakles said. "But would you at least help me adjust my position so I can be more comfortable? After all, I was not expecting to have to hold the sky for long."

Atlas agreed. He placed the three apples on the ground and held the heavens up so Herakles could settle into a more comfortable position. But as he did so, Herakles rolled away from Atlas and the heavens, grabbing the three golden apples and leaving the mighty Titan to burden his punishment once more.

Atlas and the Hesperides
https://commons.wikimedia.org/wiki/File:Lucas_Cranach_d.%C3%84._-_Herkules_und_Atlas_(Herzog_Anton_Ulrich-Museum).jpg

Herakles returned to Argos, and King Eurystheus was not happy to see that Herakles had succeeded in completing another impossible task. However, rather than letting the cruel, cowardly king keep the golden fruits, Herakles gave them to Athena, who returned them to the garden.

Herakles's twelfth labor was perhaps his most perilous yet.

"I want you to go to the underworld," King Eurystheus said, barely holding back a smirk. "And bring me its guardian, Cerberus, the three-headed hound. Bring him back to me alive."

Herakles hesitated. He knew such a task would be impossible. How could he go to the underworld, take its guardian, and then come back to the land of the living? Such things could not be done! But had he not done the impossible eleven times already? Perhaps if the gods were merciful, he could pull off a twelfth miracle.

"Very well," Herakles said. "I'll bring you Cerberus."

Before going to the underworld, Herakles set off for Athens. He knew he could be initiated into the Eleusinian Mysteries. These sacred rites were conducted in honor of the goddess Demeter and her daughter, the goddess Persephone. These rites would give Herakles the ability to walk to the afterlife and then back to the mortal realm. What those rituals, ceremonies, or deeds were, we will never know for sure. The practice of the Eleusinian Mysteries was a secret to all but those who were initiated into the cult.

After Herakles acquired this mysterious knowledge, he set off for the underworld. He was escorted by Athena and the god Hermes, herald of the gods and protector of travelers, thieves, and merchants.

First, Herakles was greeted by Charon, the Ferryman, who ferried souls across the River Styx as long as they paid the fee. Herakles did not have coins with him, but after an explanation, Charon allowed the mortal man to board his boat.

Once the River Styx was crossed, Herakles was greeted by Hades himself. As Herakles had done numerous times before, he explained his predicament and the task asked of him.

Hades was terribly amused by the tale and the fact he was requesting to take his dog out to the world of the living.

"Very well," said Hades. "You may take Cerberus with you if you manage to overpower him without using any of your weapons."

Herakles looked at the giant three-headed beast that guarded the gates of the underworld. Each of his heads had sharp teeth that could easily tear through a man's flesh.

Herakles tossed aside his club and sword. He undid his belt and laid down his shield. With nothing but his bare hands, he charged at Cerberus.

The three-headed hound easily evaded Herakles's first attack, proving himself to be not just powerful but also intelligent. Hades watched on with mild curiosity. Getting the lay of the land, Herakles cornered Cerberus by the River Acheron, leaving the hound no escape route. Herakles charged forward once more, and with his mighty strength, he overpowered Cerberus, wrestling and holding him down until he became docile.

A 16ᵗʰ-century engraving of Herakles capturing Cerberus.
https://commons.wikimedia.org/wiki/File:Hercules_Capturing_Cerberus_LACMA_47.31.158.jpg

Hades applauded Herakles's fight and gave him permission to leave. Carrying the three-headed hound on his shoulders, Herakles returned to the mortal world and headed straight to Argos.

King Eurystheus trembled with fear as soon as he laid eyes on Cerberus. Falling to his knees, he begged Herakles to release the hellish beast. With a smirk, Herakles did as King Eurystheus asked, and Cerberus returned to the underworld.

"I have completed all twelve labors you set out for me to do. Though they were impossible, I finished each and every one of them. I have earned my penance. I have atoned for the cruel murder of my beloved wife and young sons."

"Yes," King Eurystheus said, unable to deny the truth. "Yes, you have. And you are now free of your servitude. Go, and let me never see you again."

And so it was that Herakles spent twelve years atoning for his sin, but through those twelve labors, he cleansed his soul and proved his might. Many say that after this trial, he earned his godhood. Others say that it took many more adventures before he was granted immortality. Regardless of how his story goes continues, these were the Twelve Labors of Herakles.

Activity 4: Timeline

Number Herakles's twelve labor in the correct order.

( ) Slay the Stymphalian Birds

( ) Capture Artemis's Ceryneian Hind

( ) Retrieve Hippolyta's Belt

( ) Slay and skin the Nemean Lion

( ) Steal three golden apples from the Hesperides' garden

( ) Bring Cerberus to the mortal realm alive

( ) Slay the Lernaean Hydra

( ) Clean the Augean Stables

( ) Bring Geryon's Cattle

( ) Capture the Cretan Bull

( ) Capture the Erymanthian Boar alive

( ) Steal the Mares of Diomedes

Chapter 5: Jason and the Argonauts

It is sometimes said that few Greek heroes meet a happy ending. Either due to their fatal flaws—most often pride—or the whims of the gods, the names that were revered and immortalized by mythology also served as cautionary stories with lessons that we should all take to heart.

The great hero Jason is not an exception to this rule. When first hearing of his life, many would be surprised at the dark turns it takes. What begins as an adventurous narrative of brotherhood, with heroes crossing the high seas and facing incredible perils to fulfill a quest, turns into a gruesome, bloody tale. This tale has a lackluster ending, something that people of ancient Greece would have dreaded more than a painful, torturous death.

We begin this story with the events preceding Jason's birth.

There was once a king named Cretheus who ruled over the land of Iolcus. He named his son, Aeson, as his heir, but when Cretheus died, Aeson's half-brother, Pelias, usurped the throne. He threw Aeson in prison. Aeson learned that his half-brother intended to kill him, so he took his own life, not wanting to give his tormentor the satisfaction of killing him.

Aeson was married to the young, beautiful, and intelligent Alcimede, a descendant of the god Hermes. Alcimede was pregnant with Aeson's son and heir. Once Aeson died, this young boy would become the rightful heir to the throne of Iolcus.

Grieving for her beloved husband and fearing for her child's life, Alcimede managed to convince her attendants to hide the newborn so that his life would be spared. When Pelias barged into the delivery room, demanding to see the baby, the attendants shook their heads.

"He is dead, my lord," they said, sounding as remorseful as possible. "The child was stillborn. He didn't even draw a breath. He came out of the womb as if he were asleep."

Believing the threat to his reign had been managed, Pelias left without demanding to see the infant's corpse or arranging for a funeral. As soon as he left, the attendants gave the mother her baby, and she cradled him in her arms.

"It's not safe for you here," Alcimede told the child as if he could understand her. "As long as that tyrant lives, your life will be in constant danger. I must protect you, even if that means having you away from me."

Alcimede named her child Jason, and she sent him away to Chiron, knowing that the wise centaur would be able to properly prepare Jason to defend himself against Pelias should the man ever find out his nephew was still alive.

The years passed, and Jason grew into a strong and handsome young man. The years passed, and Pelias continued to be king of Iolcus. He was a tyrant to his people. He was also paranoid that someone would take his throne from him, just as he had taken the throne from his brother.

Pelias often relied on the wisdom of the Oracle, and he would always ask her about potential threats to his throne. She spoke nothing. One day, though, a prophecy was made.

"You must be aware of the man with one sandal," said the Oracle. "He will be the one responsible for your undoing."

Desperate to avoid his own end, Pelias prayed to the gods, pleading for their help and sacrificing the best cattle in their honor. Pelias prayed, pleaded, and honored every single Olympian except for one: Hera, the goddess of marriage, women, and family. Such an oversight naturally offended the prideful goddess. She decided that Pelias must pay for this insult, and Jason would be the instrument with which she would get her revenge.

Time passed, and Pelias held some athletic games in honor of Poseidon. By now, Jason was well trained and ready to leave his mentor behind. He was eager to face the world on his own and make a name for himself. When word of the competition reached his ear, he decided to bid Chiron goodbye and go to Iolcus.

On his way, Jason met a helpless old woman who was trying to cross the River Anauros. He approached her with a smile.

"My lady, I see you are having some trouble crossing the river," he said. "I am strong and young. I would be happy to assist you should you request my services."

"How kind of you, young man," the old lady said. "Yes, I would very much like assistance crossing this river."

Carrying the old woman on his back, Jason crossed the river with little difficulty. However, he lost one of his sandals, which was washed away by the time he reached the other side of the water.

He thought nothing of it and gently placed the old woman on the ground.

"Here you are," Jason said. "If you don't mind me asking, where are you going? Perhaps you would like an escort to see you safely to your final destination?"

"Do not worry about that, young man," the old lady said. "But for your help, I shall give you a blessing from the gods. You are young and strong, and men like you often make enemies of dishonorable tyrants. You will face many hardships in your life, but know that the gods will be by your side."

Jason thanked the old woman for her blessing, and the two parted ways. Of course, Jason did not know the old lady was the goddess Hera in disguise. By giving him her blessing, she had proclaimed him a favorite of hers.

As soon as Jason arrived in Iolcus to compete in the game, Pelias realized he was the one whom the prophecy spoke of. He confronted Jason. Jason knew he was the rightful heir to the throne and revealed his identity.

Pelias seeing Jason with only one sandal.

https://commons.wikimedia.org/wiki/File:Pelias_meets_Jason_MAN_Napoli_Inv111436.jpg

"You killed my father. My mother was forced to send me far from my home to protect me," Jason declared. "I have now returned to Iolcus and intend to compete in these games and take back what is rightfully mine."

Pelias was scared. He knew he could not win a fight against Jason, who was much younger and much fitter than he was. But he still wished to avoid a gruesome death.

"You wish to take the throne for yourself?" Pelias asked. "Very well, nephew. I will not fight you. But you are still a young man. You have no deeds associated with your name. Don't you think the people of Iolcus deserve a better king than a young boy fresh from training?"

Jason frowned. "What do you mean? If you're trying to insult me—"

"Not at all! I simply mean that perhaps you need to prove to your people that you are worthy to be their king," Pelias said. "Go on a quest. Prove your worth. Then, when you return, I shall give you the throne."

"Very well. What is this quest you speak of?"

Pelias smirked. "Your quest, Jason, son of Aeson, is to bring me the Golden Fleece."

Jason did not hesitate to accept it.

Before we talk about Jason's journey to find the Golden Fleece, we must first explain what it is, how it came to be, and why it was so coveted.

There once was a king named Athamas who ruled over Boeotia. He married a cloud nymph named Nephele. They had twins, a boy named Phrixus and a girl named Helle. Eventually, Athamas fell in love with another, a woman named Ino, who was the daughter of Cadmus.

Nephele was offended, and she left Athamas and Boeotia. Her children remained with their father, even after he took a new wife. After Nephele left, a never-ending drought took hold of the land, leading to failing crops and starvation.

Ino grew envious of the two children, and she decided to have them murdered. She convinced her husband that the only way to end the drought was to sacrifice the two children to Poseidon. Ino went as far as to bribe the Oracle to lie to her husband and the people of Boeotia. The Oracle told the people that Ino was right and that only the way to stop the drought was to kill the twins.

But Nephele was still watching out for her children, and she sent a golden ram to rescue them from the sacrifice. They rode on the ram's back as it crossed the Black Sea. Tragically, Helle fell from the back of the ram and drowned. The spot where Helle died was once known as the Hellespont. Today, it is known as the Strait of Gallipoli or the Dardanelles.

The ram and Phrixus reached Colchis, where they were welcomed by King Aeetes. Now, while you may not know Aeetes's name, you may be familiar with his father, Helios, and his two sisters, Pasiphae (the mother of the Minotaur) and the witch Circe (who played a role in Odysseus's journey home after the Trojan War). King Aeetes had three children: two daughters named Medea and Chalciope and his young son and heir, Absyrtus. Remember these names; they will appear later on in our tale.

Now, King Aeetes saw that Phrixus and his daughter, Chalciope, had fallen in love. He gave them permission to wed. To thank Aeetes for allowing him to marry his daughter and for welcoming him into his home, Phrixus gave Aeetes the golden ram. The ram was sacrificed, and its golden wool—the Golden Fleece—was hung on an oak in a grove sacred to the god Ares. The fleece was also guarded by a dragon.

While you might have never of this story before, you have certainly come across its imagery before. The golden ram is the same ram depicted by the zodiac sign and constellation of Aries.

Jason would have been familiar with parts of this story. He knew where to find it, and he also knew that such a perilous journey could not be accomplished alone.

And so, after accepting Pelias's quest, Jason set out to find companions for this journey. He gathered a crew of fifty men, all of whom were just as strong, young, and eager to make a name for themselves as Jason was. Among them were Herakles, whose tale of his twelve labors is featured in this collection, and the famous Orpheus, a musician whose descent into the underworld to save his beloved Eurydice is remembered as a cautionary tale of faith and trust. There were also Peleus, whose son Achilles would become a hero in the Trojan War, and Erginus, a son of Poseidon, who was said to be able to walk on water. And, of course, we cannot forget the virgin huntress Atalanta, who was a beloved friend of the goddess Artemis.

Together, this crew became known as the Argonauts, named after their majestic ship, the *Argo*. The ship was named after its builder, Argus. It was said that the *Argo* was the fastest galley to ever cross the Black Sea. Athena helped design the vessel. Its bow was crafted out of an oak belonging to Zeus's oracle at Dodona. These divine features were said to instill the ship with powers that made those who looked upon it see a gigantic monster instead of a ship.

A painting of the Argo by Konstantinos Volanakis.
https://commons.wikimedia.org/wiki/File:Constantine_Volanakis_Argo.jpg

And so, Jason and the Argonauts set off through the Black Sea to retrieve the famed Golden Fleece.

At the time this tale takes place, such long journeys could not be made in one go. The crew needed to stop frequently. Such stops were often the source of trouble. Heroes faced many obstacles they had to overcome to reach their destination. Jason and the Argonauts were no exception.

Their first stop was the island of Lemnos. The Argonauts did not know this at the time, but the island was populated solely by women. Long ago, men walked its lands. However, the women offended the goddess Aphrodite by failing to worship her properly. She cursed the women to have a stench so foul that none of the men would come near them. The men looked for companionship elsewhere, betraying their wives and abandoning their families. Furious, the women murdered all of the men, and they now lived under the rule of Queen Hypsipyle.

When the *Argo* reached Lemnos, her crew was welcomed with a feast. Queen Hypsipyle promised Jason that he and his crew were welcome to stay as long as they wished.

Jason and his crew stayed in Lemnos for a year. The celebrations and the entertainment made them forget their quest. Many of the men took the women of Lemnos as their consorts and had children with them. Jason slept on Hypsipyle's bed, and they had twins. One can only assume that Aphrodite's curse had worn off.

The only ones who resisted such temptation were Herakles, his lover, Hylas, and a few others. Rather than joining in the festivities at Lemnos, they stayed in the *Argo*, waiting for sense to come back to their companions so they could resume their quest.

But as the year lapsed, Herakles realized his friends would not remember their purpose. He marched to Jason, his disgust and fury clear.

"Have you no shame?" Herakles demanded. "Have you forgotten why you gathered us together and why we set sail?"

Jason blinked at Herakles, confused. "What do you mean?"

"I mean that you seem to have forgotten our purpose. Either that or you have no intention of fulfilling our quest," Herakles said. "If that is the case, tell me now. I'll leave with my men, and you and the others can stay here for an eternity."

"Herakles, please—"

"No! You were entrusted with a quest. You said retrieving the Golden Fleece would prove you are worthy of being the king of Iolcus," Herakles said. "Have you given up on that already? Is Pelias, the man who stole the throne, to wear your crown forever? It's been a year since our arrival, and you have shown no signs of being ready to leave."

Jason sighed. He nodded solemnly, ashamed.

"You are right. We lost sight of our purpose. We stayed here for far too long," Jason said. "Thank you, my friend. This quest would have been lost without you."

And so, Jason and the Argonauts left Lemnos.

They next stopped at land whose people were known as the Dolionians. Their king went by the name Cyzicus. The Dolionians welcomed the Argonauts to their home, offering them shelter and welcoming them to gather any supplies they might need for their journey ahead.

"You may stay as long as you need," said King Cyzicus. "And we will make you comfortable and merry. Rest now, for the journey ahead of you is long."

Jason thanked the king for his hospitality. He and the Argonauts rested and made themselves comfortable among the Dolionians. They soon went to the forest to gather supplies.

Although King Cyzicus was a welcoming host, he neglected to tell the Argonauts that his people were not the only ones who lived in that land. Beyond Bear Mountain, there were six-armed giants known as the Gegenees. They had been terrorizing the Dolionians for years.

When the Gegenees saw the *Argo*, they figured that it must carry a lot of precious cargo. So, they decided to raid it. Unfortunately for them, and fortunately for Jason, Herakles and a handful of men had remained behind to guard the ship. As soon as they saw the giants running toward them, they pulled out their swords.

"Defend the *Argo*!" cried Herakles. "Do not let any of these monsters survive!"

A fierce battle broke out. Herakles and his men somehow managed to do the impossible, killing the majority of the Gegenees, despite their greater size, strength, and number of limbs. The few survivors were so terrified of the son of Zeus that they ran back to the mountains, never to bother King Cyzicus and his people again.

"I cannot believe this," said King Cyzicus. "We've been terrorized by those monsters for generations. No hero has ever managed to drive them off like that. For that, you have our eternal gratitude."

A celebratory feast was held in honor of Herakles and the Argonauts who fought off the Gegenees. They celebrated for days. Jason and his crew took as many supplies as they could carry. Finally, it came time to leave the Dolionians and return to their quest.

Well, at least that was the plan. Only a few hours into their sailing, the *Argo* was caught in a terrible storm. Jason and his crew tried to keep the ship steady, but the waves kept pushing them back. Night fell, and they still struggled to maintain their ship. Finally, they were driven to a dark beach.

The Argonauts didn't realize the storm had pushed them back to the Dolionians' lands. King Cyzicus and his men did not realize that the ship was not filled with raiders. Determined to defend their shores, they pulled out their swords and charged. The Argonauts were determined to defend themselves against the attackers. They also pulled out their swords and met bronze with bronze.

A battle ensued. In the dark, no one could tell that they were fighting friends. Men fell to the ground, their blood soaking the sand, their wounds washed by the salty waves. As dawn began to break and the first vestiges of pale light illuminated the sky, the Dolionians saw they were attacking the Argonauts. The Argonauts saw they were attacking the Dolionians.

The fight immediately stopped. No grudge was held, and they gathered their dead. It was then that they realized King Cyzicus was among the fallen. It was impossible to know whose blade had taken his life.

They held a joint funeral for all of those who lost their life. Cyzicus's wife was so struck by grief that she hung herself.

When the Argonauts left this time, it was with a heavy heart. The sky was clear at least, so they were able to navigate the waters.

There was still a long way to go until they could reach Colchis. Their next stop would perhaps cause them their biggest loss.

They next stopped in Pegea to rest and eat. That was when Herakles's beloved Hylas, who was eager to stretch his legs after a long journey, wandered around the forest. He explored the land with the curiosity one only finds in youths.

He came across a beautiful spring with sweet water. The spring was surrounded by lush green bushes and shaded by great trees.

After removing his clothes, Hylas entered the water. He washed away the salt from his skin. He drank some of the water to calm his thirst. And he swam to cool himself from the heat. As he was getting to return to his friends, he heard the distinct sound of giggling.

"Who goes there?" he demanded. He looked around and saw nothing. "Show yourself!"

The giggling continued, but Hylas still could see no one.

"I know you're there," he said, louder this time. "I can hear you! If you intend no ill, then you have no reason to hide."

The giggling did not stop, but Hylas finally could see its source. Beautiful water nymphs, known as Naiads, appeared around the spring. They smiled at Hylas and batted their eyelashes.

"No need to be so rude, beautiful hero," they said. "We mean no harm."

"My apologies," Hylas said. "I did not mean to cause offense."

"Apology accepted," they said, entering the water. "Under the condition you swim with us for a little while longer."

Hylas frowned. "I really shouldn't. I need to go back to my ship and to Herakles."

"A little while longer won't make a difference," they said, swimming toward him. "Please? You made yourself comfortable in our spring. You drank our water, and you washed yourself. The least you can do is play with us a little, oh beautiful hero."

Hylas was still hesitant, but the Naiads were by his side. Their fingers wrapped around his wrist in a gentle grip, and they giggled as they encouraged him to come deeper and deeper into the water.

"Just a little while longer, beautiful hero."

Hylas and the Nymphs

https://commons.wikimedia.org/wiki/File:Waterhouse_Hylas_Nymphs_study.jpg

By this point, Hylas was too weak to resist the Naiads' charm. He followed them into the water, and they laughed, delighted. For a moment, their play was as innocent as that of children swimming together under the summer sun.

One of the Naiads approached Hylas. She wrapped her arms around his shoulders, pressing her body against his.

"Oh, beautiful hero. You won't leave us, will you?"

Hylas looked around and saw that the other Naiads had surrounded him.

"You won't leave us, beautiful hero. Because we won't let you."

And together, all of the Naiads pulled Hylas under the water.

Herakles was beginning to worry over his favorite companion's whereabouts. He knew Hylas was a capable fighter, having taught him much during their time together. But he also knew that Hylas was not the type to spend this long away from him, especially in an unfamiliar land with unknown dangers.

"I'm going to search for Hylas," Herakles told Jason. "I'll be back as soon as I find him."

But Herakles could not find him. He searched for Hylas all day and all night. When noon came the next day, he still saw no sign of his beloved friend. With each passing minute, his worry grew. He was certain that something horrible had happened to Hylas.

Finally, it came time for the *Argo* to leave.

"I cannot go," Herakles said. "Not without Hylas."

"Are you certain, Herakles?" Jason asked. "If you haven't found him yet, there's a chance you never will."

"I won't give up. I'm not leaving this place until I find him."

"Then we'll stay with you," Jason said.

But Herakles shook his head.

"No. Go, my friend. You have your quest to fulfill, and you do not need me for it. I have to find Hylas. I'm afraid this is the place where our paths must part."

"Very well."

Herakles and Jason wished each other luck and bid farewell. The *Argo* left without the mightiest Argonaut. Herakles would never see Hylas again. Jason's path would be filled with more peril and darkness than he could have ever imagined.

Their next stop was Salmydessus in Thrace. Their king, Phineus, was a blind seer. He had been given the gift of prophecy by Apollo. However, in his telling of the future, he greatly offended Zeus, who punished him for the insult.

"Welcome, great heroes," King Phineus said once Jason and the Argonauts came to his palace. "I hope you enjoy your stay in Salmydessus."

Jason and the Argonauts could see that there was something wrong with the king. He appeared ill. His skin was too pale, and his body was too frail. But they held their tongue, not wanting to offend their host.

"We thank you for your hospitality, Your Majesty," said Jason. "And if there's anything we can do to help, please do not hesitate to ask."

"In fact, there is something you can do for me," King Phineus said. "And in return, I shall give you something as well."

It was then that King Phineus told Jason and the Argonauts about the punishment inflicted on him. Every time he sat down for a meal, Harpies—monsters who were half-human and half-bird, known by some as "the hounds of Zeus"—would come down and make a mess out of it.

"Even if I try to eat a peach in the privacy of my chambers, the Harpies will still fly in and steal it from my hand before I can even take a bite," King Phineus said. "As you can see, I'm withering away. I am not sure how much longer I can last."

The Argonauts were horrified by the story and promised to help King Phineus. The king told them that in his vision, the sons of Boreas, the North Wind, were the ones who would save him from his torment.

That was when two of the Argonauts stepped up from the crowd. Their names were Calais and Zetes, and they were known as the Boreads (the wind brothers).

"We'll be happy to be of assistance, Your Majesty," said the brothers.

And so, a plan was devised. During a feast, Calais and Zetes stood guard by King Phineus, one on each side. Sure enough, as soon as a plate of food was placed in front of the king, the Harpies came down, stealing the food. They spit on what little remained, making it so foul that even the heroes could not hide their disgust.

But rather than let the Harpies fly away, the wind brothers chased them, their swords drawn. They caught up with the Harpies and fought them. They were ready to strike a killing blow when Iris, the goddess of the rainbow, ordered them to stop. The Harpies were servants of Zeus, and killing them would infuriate the god. She promised the Harpies would torment King Phineus no more.

As a sign of gratitude, King Phineus gave Jason and the Argonauts some words of wisdom.

"Your goal is to reach Colchis, is it not?" King Phineus asked. "You are after the Golden Fleece?"

"Yes, that is our quest."

"You must be careful. While your journey to Colchis will soon come to an end, you are about to face the most perilous part of your travels," King Phineus said. "To get to Colchis, you'll have to pass through the Symplegades."

The Symplegades, also known as the Clashing Rocks, marked the entrance to the Black Sea. These rocks were made of granite and one hundred times as long as they were tall. They were said to be the guardians of the region. Whenever a vessel tried to pass through the rocks, they would snap shut, killing every living thing between them. The motion was so violent and aggressive that it created fierce waves. Not even Poseidon's mightiest sea creature could overcome them. A wise crew would travel around them, but unfortunately for Jason and the Argonauts, there was no way to reach Colchis without passing through that strait.

"Take a dove with you," instructed King Phineus. "And just as you are about to approach the rocks, release it. It will fly between the rocks, and the rocks will snap shut. You'll be able to see how fast you must go to successfully cross the Symplegades."

Jason and the Argonauts thanked King Phineus for his help and wisdom. They stayed in Salmydessus for a few more days before departing on their journey once again, dove in hand.

They approached the Symplegades. Though King Phineus had warned them of their might, no words could have prepared the crew for the magnificent sight in front of them. The rocks were taller than tall and longer than long. The sides faced each other perfectly vertical.

The crew slowed down the *Argo*, going as close as possible while also keeping a safe distance. Then Jason released the dove. Just as King Phineus said, the dove flew between the rocks. They started to vibrate. Then, they snapped shut. But the dove flew faster than the Symplegades, making it safely to the other side while only losing a feather.

The Argonauts facing the Symplegades.
https://commons.wikimedia.org/wiki/File:Symplegades,_illustration_for_The_Heroes.jpg

Jason observed this and calculated how fast they would need to row. The Argonauts looked at each other, apprehensive. Orpheus, who used drums to beat the rhythm for the oarsmen, took a deep breath. At Jason's signal, they started making their way through the Symplegades.

Never before and never again did the *Argo* sail so fast. The oarsmen rowed with all their might, ignoring the pain in their muscles, struggling to see through the sweat that rolled down their faces.

Yet even their best might not have been enough to get through this. Seeing their predicament, the goddess Athena used her divine powers to hold the rocks back so that the *Argo* would have enough time to make it through the straits. As soon as they were safely out, the goddess's strength gave out, and the rocks snapped shut, never to be opened again.

And so, Jason and the Argonauts finally made it to Colchis.

There, they were received by King Aeetes, his daughter Medea, and his young son and heir, Apysrtus, who was still only a child.

"Welcome, Jason of Iolcus," said the king. "I imagine your journey to our land was long and perilous. You must be exhausted."

"Indeed, it was, Your Majesty, and indeed we are," said Jason. "But we are determined to complete our quest."

"Yes, yes. But we can discuss the matters of your quest later," King Aeetes said. "For now, let us feast, and let your men rest. Tomorrow, we shall discuss how I may assist you on your quest."

Jason and the Argonauts thanked King Aeetes for his hospitality. They feasted and rested, but they did not know that King Aeetes had no intention of helping them get the Golden Fleece. You see, long ago, King Aeetes had heard a prophecy that Jason would be the one to bring about the fall of Colchis.

To prevent that from happening, the king decided he would give Jason three impossible tasks to complete before he was allowed to take the Golden Fleece. The cunning king hoped these tasks would kill the hero and prevent tragedy from striking his kingdom.

When Jason heard of these three tasks, he accepted them bravely, though inside, he worried. What sort of challenges did Aeetes hold in store for him? Jason knew they would be deadly in nature since the king would try anything to keep the Golden Fleece.

"How am I supposed to do this? I'll die for sure! Oh, gods, what should I do?"

Hera listened to her champion's worries and went to Aphrodite for help. Together, the two goddesses created a charm that would make its recipient fall madly in love with the giver.

"We heard your pleas for guidance and help, Jason. We are here with the answer to your woes," Hera said.

"Take this charm, and give it to Princess Medea," said Aphrodite. "When she receives it, she will fall madly in love with you. She will do everything in her power to help you complete those tasks and get the Golden Fleece."

Medea as painted by Anselm Feuerbach
https://commons.wikimedia.org/wiki/File:Medea_an_der_Urne.jpg

Jason thanked the two goddesses and followed their instructions. Sure enough, as soon as Medea received the charm, the attraction she already felt toward the hero intensified, becoming an all-consuming love. Just as the goddesses had predicted, Medea vowed to do whatever was in her power to help Jason, even if that meant turning against her own father.

Now, Medea was not just a regular princess. She was a priestess of the goddess Hecate, the goddess of witchcraft. Like her aunt Circe, she was a powerful sorceress. She was a great ally and an even more dangerous enemy, but she was determined to use her magic to assist Jason.

"Now, Jason, if you insist on continuing with this quest, you will have to complete the three tasks I assign to you," said King Aeetes. "Do you still wish to go forward with this?"

Jason looked at Medea, who nodded at him.

"I do."

"Very well," said King Aeetes. "Your first task is to plow a field with the Khalkotauroi."

Jason accepted the task without hesitation.

Now, the Khalkotauroi were large fire-breathing bulls that were given to Aeetes by Hephaestus, the god of blacksmiths and craftsmen. Unknown to King Aeetes, Medea knew what task he would give Jason. The previous night, she had told him about her father's plan while also giving him a magic potion.

"This will protect you from the fire," she told Jason. "Spread it through your body as if it were an ointment. Once you are invulnerable to their fire, the Khalkotauroi will be just like any other bull."

Jason did as Medea instructed him the previous night. Sure enough, when the bulls breathed fire in their direction, the flames brushed against his skin as if they were water. Jason could not even feel their heat. He then used his great strength to tame the two bulls and easily plowed a field, just as King Aeetes had requested.

"You did well with your first task, Jason," said King Aeetes. "But you'll find that your second one will not be so easy."

"I would be disappointed if it wasn't," said Jason.

"Very well. For your second task, I want you to sow the field you just plowed with dragon teeth."

Once more, Jason accepted the task without hesitation. And once more, Medea knew what her father had planned. She instructed Jason on how to best overcome this obstacle.

"When you sink the dragon teeth into the ground, Spartoi will rise from the soil," Medea said. "You must confuse them. This way, they'll attack each other, taking themselves down. Then you can easily defeat whoever is left."

Spartoi, whose name literally means "sown men," were great warriors that would spring up from the ground whenever dragon teeth were planted in the dirt. While Jason was a fierce fighter, even he could not take down a large army on his own. Medea's help spared his life.

Just as Medea had told him, as soon as Jason plunged the dragon teeth into the soil, Spartoi rose up. Quickly, before they gained awareness of their surroundings, Jason rolled a giant boulder into the middle of the field. This successfully confused the warriors, and they attacked one another until only five remained. Jason was able to overcome them with ease.

"Well done, Jason," said King Aeetes. "You have completed two tasks already."

"Yes. And I plan to complete the third one as well."

"Are you sure this is what you wish? You still have time to abandon this foolish errand."

"Tell me the third task, Your Majesty."

"Very well," said King Aeetes. "You want to take the Golden Fleece with you to Iolcus, do you not? Fine. If that is your wish, then your third task is to get it yourself. If you can pass the dragon guarding the fleece and grab it, then it shall be yours."

For the third time, Jason did not hesitate to accept the task.

However, this task frightened him more than the others. He had seen the grove where the Golden Fleece was kept, and he had seen the dragon guarding it. Jason was a great warrior, but overcoming a dragon would be a challenge.

"Worry not about that, my love," Medea said. "Have your ship ready to leave. We'll go to the grove tonight, and we'll retrieve the fleece from right under the dragon's nose."

"I do not know how you plan on doing this, but you have not failed me yet," Jason said. "Thank you for all your help."

"If you wish to thank me, then take me with you when you leave Colchis," Medea said. "Let me be your wife."

"Of course. I would not think of ever marrying anyone but you, my love."

Did Jason truly mean those words? Did he love her? Or was he just using Medea? To this day, many debate whether Jason's affection was true and if it soured over time or if it never existed in the first place. Perhaps Jason just never found a good way to abandon the powerful sorceress who helped him in his quest.

Regardless of what the truth might be, at the time, Jason could not have known that these words would someday doom him to a life of misery and loneliness. But that is something that will come later in our tale.

Night fell, and just as Medea had instructed, Jason prepared the *Argo* to leave at a moment's notice. He met with the sorceress, and the two snuck into the sacred grove of Ares. The full moon was out, bathing their surroundings with its pale light. Under its gaze, the Golden Fleece glimmered beautifully.

The two hid behind a bush, their eyes watching the dragon that attentively watched its surroundings.

Jason unsheathed his sword.

"How do we defeat this dragon?" Jason asked. "Share with me your wisdom, and I shall follow your advice as I have done every time."

Medea smiled. She put her hand on Jason's wrist, lowering his sword.

"We defeat it by not facing it at all," Medea said. She then showed him a vial she had brought with her. "As soon as the dragon gets a sniff of this, it will fall into a deep slumber. I'll keep it under my enchantment, giving you plenty of time to fetch the fleece and get to safety."

"Are you certain it will work?"

"Have my plans failed you yet, Jason?" Medea asked. "Trust me when I say I know what I'm doing."

Jason nodded. "You're right. I trust you."

Medea stood up and made her way to the middle of the grove. Jason held his breath. The dragon saw her, but perhaps because it was familiar with the princess, it did not attack. Rather, it approached her with suspicious curiosity. That was when Medea pulled out her vial and removed the lid. She pursed her lips and softly blew over the lid's opening.

As soon as the dragon smelled the potion's scent, its eyes grew hazy and heavy. It blinked, trying to remain conscious, but that was a losing battle. Soon, it fell asleep.

Jason waited a full five minutes before leaving the bush. Medea remained in the center of the grove, still holding her sleeping potion, as Jason grabbed the Golden Fleece and then carefully left the grove. Medea waited until he was a safe distance away to follow him.

That very same night, Jason and the Argonauts waited for Medea at the *Argo*. They were about to leave without her when Medea showed up with her little brother, Apysrtus. When Jason asked why she was bringing him, Medea only pleaded for him to trust her.

Perhaps Jason should not have done so. Perhaps many innocent lives would have been spared if he demanded Apysrtus stay behind. Perhaps much misery, suffering, and bloodshed could have been avoided. But Jason trusted Medea, and so he nodded. Medea and Apysrtus boarded the *Argo*.

As they sailed away into the night, they watched as King Aeetes finally realized what had happened. He rallied his men and began pursuing Jason and the Argonauts. That was when Medea turned to her little brother and plunged a knife into his heart, killing him instantly.

"What are you doing?" Jason demanded, horrified.

"Making sure my father doesn't follow us."

The Golden Fleece

With a terrible coldness, Medea proceeded to cut off her little brother's head, his arms, and his legs. She tossed each piece overboard so that it would float among the waves. When one of the pieces floated to Aeetes, he let out an anguished cry.

"My son! My little boy! My sweet Apysrtus!" He held the piece to his heart, sobbing, not caring that his clothes were now covered in blood. "Stop! Stop chasing them! Get my little boy's body! Retrieve every single piece so that he may be put to rest properly!"

King Aeetes's men stopped chasing the *Argo*. Instead, they now searched for the pieces of the little prince's corpse.

Jason, Medea, and the Argonauts had successfully retrieved the Golden Fleece and could now return to Colchis. And just as you might imagine, this is the point when our adventurous tale becomes grim.

Just as they had faced many obstacles traveling to Colchis, they faced many obstacles on their way back to Iolcus. The first of these was the Sirens by the sharp, rocky islands of Sirenum Scopuli.

You might have heard of Sirens before. Though many confuse them with mermaids, the Sirens looked more like birds than fish. Some claim they had the heads of women while the rest of their bodies looked like birds. Others say they were beautiful and alluring with a human female body. But they had giant wings that allowed them to fly into the sky. Regardless of their appearance, most accounts agree the Sirens were dangerous. They lived by Sirenum Scopuli and attracted sailors with their seductive songs, luring them to their deaths.

Luckily for the Argonauts, the first of their crew to hear their song was Orpheus. Some claimed he received his musical prowess because of divine parentage, either from Apollo or the Muse Calliope. As soon as the legendary singer realized what was happening and where they were, he pulled out his lyre and began playing and singing the most beautiful and loudest song he could think of.

Sure enough, Orpheus's playing was so enchanting and loud that it drowned out the Sirens' spell. No one fell prey to their song, and the *Argo* was able to safely pass by Sirenum Scopuli without losing a single crewmate.

After successfully evading the Sirens, the *Argo* stopped at Crete. Though they hoped to have a peaceful stay, they were soon faced with the Talos.

The Talos was a gigantic bronze automaton created by Hephaestus. He gifted it to Minos to guard his island against pirates and invaders. The self-moving machine was said to be at least thirty meters in height. It was filled with ichor, the golden blood of the gods, which was kept inside his form by a single nail on the nape of his neck.

As soon as the Talos saw the *Argo* approaching in the distance, it reached for boulders and flung them at the ship. Though it missed, his attacks caused the waters to grow violent, becoming nearly impossible to navigate.

"We can't keep doing this forever," Jason said. "The waters are too rough to escape, and if we stay here, it will only be a matter of time before that giant creature manages to hit the *Argo*."

"Then we won't try to escape, and we won't stay here," said Medea. "Get us closer to the automaton. I have a way to defeat it."

"Are you sure? If you're wrong, it could end up costing all our lives!"

"Have my plans failed you yet, Jason?" Medea asked. "Trust me when I say I know what I'm doing."

Jason hesitated. Undoubtedly, he thought about the last time Medea had a plan. It involved spilling innocent blood. But then, the Talos threw another boulder, this one nearly hitting the ship. A giant wave crashed on the decks, nearly sweeping some of the crew into the rough waters. They needed a solution quickly. What other choice did Jason have than to trust Medea?

"Fine," Jason said. "We'll get you close to the Talos. Do what you must to help us survive this."

Jason ordered the oarsmen to row faster and to get as close to the Talos as possible. Though the men were skeptical, they followed his orders. Medea stood on the deck, her shoulders drawn back, her chin raised.

Medea closed her eyes. She muttered something under her breath, the words falling from her lips in a constant loop. Just as the Talos was getting ready to throw another huge boulder at the *Argo*, the air chilled. A mist that should not exist surrounded the ship and the giant automaton. The Argonauts drew in their breaths, the hair on the back of their necks now standing. Something didn't feel right. No, something felt worse than not right. Something felt evil, violent, and forbidden.

A loud, ear-piercing shriek split the air. The men covered their ears. The Talos did as well. Only Medea stayed composed. However, her stillness seemed sinister rather than confident.

That was when the first Ker appeared. She swooped down from the sky, flying around the Talos's head. Then, more Keres appeared. These were female death spirits. They were daughters of Nyx, the night, and Erebus, the darkness. They came from the underworld. Their name means "doom," and they were said to be attracted to violent, painful deaths. The Keres were said to be like vultures, waiting for humans to die so they could feast on the miserable dead.

They swirled around the Talos, screeching their unholy cry. They could not kill it, but their presence was unnerving. The Talos could not bat them away. In trying to fight them off, the Talos slipped.

Some say that was enough to dislodge the nail that kept its ichor contained, killing the Talos. Others say that Medea took the Talos's fall as an opportunity and removed the nail with her own two hands. Regardless of which version of the tale you prefer to believe, the result remains the same: once the nail was removed, the ichor was drained. The Talos was no more.

The death of the Talos

Arriving at Iolcus should have been a cause for celebration. The quest was complete, and the Golden Fleece and the throne belonged to Jason. Each of the Argonauts returned to their homes, ready to continue with their own adventures. But Jason found no cause for celebration. Jason's mother had died while he was away. Pelias remained on the throne, and his tyranny was crueler than ever. It was clear to Jason, who was wiser and more mature than when he had left on his quest, that his uncle would not willingly give up his power.

Filled with anger, grief, and a desire for revenge, Jason turned to Medea.

"You have never failed me, Medea," he said. "I do not care how you do it. Punish that tyrant for his wickedness. Make sure I have the throne that rightfully belongs to me."

Medea smiled.

"If that is what you wish, my love, then that is what I'll do for you."

Disguising herself as a priestess of Artemis, Medea infiltrated the palace. She became close to Pelias's three daughters, all of whom openly mourned what old age was doing to their beloved father.

"He can't stay awake as much as he used to anymore," said the first one. "It pains my heart to see one who was once so active struggle to stay awake throughout a feast."

"He forgets names, dates, and prayers," said the second one. "It pains my heart to talk to him and see that he does not recognize me."

"His bones ache, and his muscles betray him," said the third one. "It pains my heart to see his own body cause him so much suffering."

"Oh, what we wouldn't give to see our father restored to his youth and be happy and healthy," lamented all three sisters.

Hearing their woes, Medea approached them.

"If you truly wish to give your father back his youth, then I can help you."

The three daughters were skeptical. So, Medea invited them to meet her at night, where she would prove to them that her words were true.

When the three daughters met Medea later that night, she had an old ram and a cauldron that was filled with a special elixir. The sorceress was stirring its contents when the three young women arrived.

"I hope you do not mind that I already got started on the potion," Medea said. "It takes a while to brew."

"We do not mind," said the daughters. "You said you could show us proof of your rejuvenating magic. Well? What are you waiting for?"

Medea smiled. She pulled a knife and killed the old ram, slitting its throat until it bled out. Then she took its carcass and dumped it inside the cauldron. She stirred it three times to the left, then three times to the right, then poured out its contents on the floor.

The three women gasped. Once the elixir cleared away, they saw a young lamb walking with its bumbling limbs, full of life.

"Do you believe me now?" Medea asked.

At first, the three daughters were too shocked to say anything. Then they nodded and begged Medea to help their father.

"Very well then," Medea said. "But you must follow my instructions exactly."

The three young women did as they were told. The next day, they drugged Pelias so that he would fall into a deep slumber that night. Medea gave them the cauldron filled with the elixir. Once the preparations were made, the three daughters went to their father's bedroom. One held his right hand, and the second one held his left. The third straddled her father's body and plunged the knife into his chest again and again until blood soaked their dresses and his sheets.

The three carried the body together and dumped it inside the cauldron. Just as they saw Medea do, they stirred it three times to the left, then three times to the right. But when they poured the contents on the floor, they were not greeted by a younger version of their father. All they saw was a mutilated corpse. The elixir Medea supposedly gave them was no magical potion at all but rather a simple stew. The three daughters had not given their father back his youth. They had committed patricide (the act of a child killing their father). The throne now belonged to Jason.

But of course, things could not remain so forever. Pelias had sons. When they learned of what happened to his father, they swore to avenge him. Jason and Medea were driven from the city and went to live in exile in Corinth.

Our tale would end on a happier note if we ended it here, but there's still more to go. For a while, things seemed good. Jason and Medea had children, at least two sons and one daughter. They could have been happy together had Jason not fallen in love with the Corinthian princess, Glauce.

When Jason announced his engagement to the daughter of King Creon, Medea was furious.

"How could you do this? Aren't I the mother of your children? Am I not your wife?"

"We never married," said Jason.

"You told me I would be your wife," Medea cried. "After all these years, this is how you repay me? After all I've done for you?"

"All you've done for me?"

"I helped you with the three tasks you needed to complete to get the Golden Fleece," Medea said. "I helped you escape my father's men. I helped you get past the Talos, and I gave you the throne of Iolcus!"

"And your methods forced us into exile!" Jason shot back.

"You should be thanking me for all that I did for you!"

"Thanking *you*?" Jason laughed. "If I should be thanking anyone, it is Hera and Aphrodite for making you fall in love with me."

Jason left Medea, telling her that nothing she said could change his mind. He should have remembered that what made Medea such a formidable ally also made her a dangerous enemy.

Sculpture of Medea by William Wetmore Story.
William Wetmore Story, CC0, via Wikimedia Commons;
https://commons.wikimedia.org/wiki/File:Medea_MET_553.jpg

His wedding day came, and the celebrations were grand. Jason and Glauce seemed happy and in love. King Creon was proud of the match he had made for his daughter. During the feast, the three went to see the wedding gifts. Two immediately caught the eye of the king and the princess.

"Oh, look at this cloak!" said Glauce. "It is so grand, and the fabric is so soft! I must try it on!"

"This crown is beautiful," said King Creon. "It is splendid and radiant, worthy of a king of Corinth."

As Glauce wrapped herself with the cloak, King Creon put on the crown. They soon found out these were no ordinary wedding gifts.

Glauce's cloak suddenly caught on fire. She screamed and tried to take it off, but she could not unclasp it. The flames consumed her skin, melting her flesh. The heat seared into her bones and caused her agonizing pain.

King Creon tried to help his daughter, but he found himself unable to move. The crown he wore began to tighten, causing him unbearable pain. He fell to his knees, trying to remove the cursed thing, but he could not. He only had enough time to see his daughter burn to death before his skull was crushed.

Jason was horrified, but Medea's revenge was not over. She was determined to cause the man who broke her heart as much pain as possible. Medea killed their two sons, brutally butchering them and leaving their corpses for Jason to find.

By the time Jason found his poor boys, Medea had long left Corinth. Her grandfather, the god Helios, gave her a dragon-pulled carriage and granted her passage to Athens.

Jason was left alone and miserable. Because he betrayed Medea, he was forsaken by Hera, the goddess of marriage, who considered his actions unforgivable. The years passed, and glory never returned to the fallen hero. He could not even be proud of his death. He died while sleeping beneath the rotten *Argo*, killed by a beam that fell from the once magnificent vessel.

Activity 5: Fill-in-the-blank Exercise

Fill in the blank spots with the correct answer from the box below.

1. The Oracle warned Pelias to beware of _____.

2. The zodiac constellation of _____ is based on the golden ram that saved the twins Phrixus and Helle from being sacrificed by their stepmother.

3. The ship Jason and his crew journeyed on was called the _____, and for this reason, they were known as the _____.

4. Herakles's lover, _____, was taken by Naiads.

5. Jason passed through the _____ by first releasing a dove. After seeing how fast they clashed, he knew at what speed to row.

6. _____ was the king of Colchis. He had three children: _____, _____, and _____.

7. To help Jason steal the Golden Fleece, Medea put _____ to sleep.

8. Orpheus saved the crew from certain death at the hands of the _____ by playing his lyre and singing.

9. The _____ was a gigantic bronze automaton created by Hephaestus and gifted to Minos to guard his island against pirates and invaders.

10. When Jason betrayed Medea to marry Glauce, Medea got her revenge by cursing a _____ and a _____ that were given to the couple as wedding gifts.

Symplegades	Crown	Dragon	*Argo*	Talos	Medea	Hylas
Aeetes	Aries	Man with One Sandal	Chalciope	Cloak	Absyrtus	Sirens	Argonauts

Chapter 6: House of Atreus

In all Greek mythology, few families are more unfortunate than the House of Atreus. Generation after generation suffered from tragedy at the hands of the Fates until they were finally freed from the curse by murder and a sibling reunion.

We begin our tale with Tantalus. He was a king and the son of Zeus. He was married to Dione, the daughter of Atlas. Tantalus was rich and greatly beloved. He was favored by the Olympians, his godly relatives, and was often invited to keep their company and dine by their side. Most humans, even those with godly blood, would have been humbled by such treatment. They knew that it was by the gods' good graces that they were blessed with such fortune.

But Tantalus was not like most humans. He let his favoritism get to his head. He grew proud and thought himself far more important than he truly was. He eventually thought of himself to be like the gods, and then he thought he was superior. He believed he could easily trick them into doing something barbaric and that he could do it with ease.

"Father, you always invite me to dine alongside you and your family," Tantalus said one day. "I would like to thank you for your hospitality by inviting you to my own palace. Let me have the honor to host all of you for once."

"That sounds splendid, my son," said Zeus, not suspecting anything to be amiss. "I'll talk to the other Olympians. Once we are all agreed, we shall meet you at your palace to dine together."

When Tantalus returned home, he put his wicked plan into motion. He ordered his son, Pelops, to be murdered. His flesh was cut into tiny pieces and mixed in with the stew. As you may well imagine, eating humans was as taboo back in those days as it is now. Tantalus just wanted to see if he could trick the gods into committing the most unholy of acts.

Finally, it came time for the feast. The gods sat at Tantalus's table. They were served the finest wine and the most aromatic bread. The most talented musicians in Tantalus's court played the best songs on their lyre. The gods drank and traded stories with Tantalus. All were merry.

The stew was brought out, and all the Olympians grew silent. They looked at one another as they were served the stew, but none made a move to eat it, with the sole exception of Demeter. The goddess was still distraught over the loss of Persephone and did not realize what she was eating. One of the gods sitting by her side quickly removed the plate from in front of her, sparing her from eating more than Pelops's shoulder.

The gods' joy turned into fury and disgust.

Zeus rose from his seat. "You dare insult us by serving this?"

Tantalus smiled. "What are you talking about, Father? It is just stew."

Zeus scoffed. "Just stew?"

"Delicious stew. Prepared by my finest cooks and made with the finest meat in all of the land."

The gods grunted in disgust.

"You would have us eat your own flesh and blood, your own son... And for what? What is the purpose of this gruesome game you play?" Zeus demanded. "Why would you commit the most unholy of acts and try to trick us into joining you in sin?"

Tantalus's smile slipped from his lips as he finally realized the severity of his predicament. He had angered and dishonored the Olympians beyond belief. As he looked at each of their faces, he knew his punishment would be as torturous as his act.

"For your actions, you shall be banished into the underworld," Zeus declared. "There, you will stand on an island surrounded by a pool of sweet water. But whenever you try to drink from it, the water shall move just out of your reach. There will be a tree on the island with you, with juicy fruit hanging from its branches. But whenever you try to reach for one of them to eat, the branches will move so that your fingertips will just brush against it. The fruit will always be out of your reach. You shall spend eternity thirsty and surrounded by water and hungry and surrounded by delicious food. There will be no way to end your torment!"

After the incident, Zeus met with the Moirai, the three Fates, and they brought young Pelops back to life. Hephaestus, the god of blacksmiths, made him a new metal shoulder. Demeter, the goddess of the harvest, presented the young man with it, for that was the part of his body that she had eaten.

For generations to come, Pelops would be the only member of the House of Atreus not to suffer another tragedy. Perhaps the Fates decided the young man had suffered enough and that he should not be punished for his father's actions.

Pelops as drawn by Guillaume Rouillé.
https://en.wikipedia.org/wiki/File:Pelops.jpg

Pelops eventually married Princess Hippodamia. Her father, King Oenomaus, was the owner of a prized racehorse, which was gifted to him by Ares, the god of war. Whenever a new suitor appeared to court his daughter, King Oenomaus would challenge them to a race. If they won, they could marry Princess Hippodamia. Since King Oenomaus's horse was superior, he won every time. And every time he won, he killed his opponent.

It just so happens that Pelops had a horse that was given to him by Poseidon. So, when he fell in love with Hippodamia and raced for her hand, he managed to win against the king. Pelops and Hippodamia married, and they had many children, though, for the purpose of this tale, we will focus on only two of them: Atreus and Thyestes. We shall discuss their unfortunate fates a little later.

Pelops's sister, Niobe, was not as fortunate. She eventually married Amphion, who was the son of Zeus. Together, they ruled over Thebes. They had seven sons and seven daughters, all of whom were beautiful and successful. For a while, Niobe's life appeared to be perfect, and that was what led to her downfall.

Like her father, Niobe took her good fortune for granted. Rather than being humble and grateful, she grew arrogant. She was certain that her achievements and her children's achievements proved her to be mightier than the gods.

Her ruin came during a festival in honor of the goddess Leto. As the people of Thebes worshiped the goddess, Niobe marched toward the center of Leto's temple and raised her arms.

"People of Thebes! Don't waste your prayers on this low-ranking goddess! I am your queen, and you should be saying your thanks to me and making sacrifices in my honor!" she boasted. "What good has Leto ever done to you? You think her superior to me, your own queen? My mother was a daughter of Atlas! My father was a son of Zeus who was welcomed at the Olympians' table! My husband built this very city you call your home! And yet it is Leto you worship? Leto, who only had two children? Why, I have six times as many children as her, and all of them are six times more worthy of your praise!"

To the ancient Greeks, few sins were more dishonorable than hubris (pride). In her declaration of superiority, Niobe angered Leto, Artemis, and Apollo. The godly twins took action against the women who dared to insult their beloved mother.

Almost as soon as the last boastful words fell from Niobe's lips, carriages descended from the sky. Artemis and Apollo were said to be the best archers of all Olympus, and they drew their bows. With six swift arrows, Artemis hit and killed all six of Niobe's daughters. With six swift arrows, Apollo hit and killed all six of Niobe's sons. Niobe watched all twelve of her children fall to their deaths, their blood soaking the ground.

Niobe fell to her knees. She did not let out an anguished cry. She did not scream. She did not beg for forgiveness or demand they be brought back to life. Rather, she remained paralyzed by grief, silent tears running down her cheeks as she stared at the twelve corpses with wide eyes.

No one could move Niobe from that spot. No one could console her or get her to respond. She remained still. She was so still that she eventually froze into stone, her grief forever carved in her features, her cheeks always damp by the tears that would fall for eternity.

Now we must leave the unfortunate Niobe to see the fate of her nephews, Pelops's two sons.

The fate of these two men and their misfortune were entangled for generations. It started with jealousy and betrayal. The older brother, Atreus, was king, and he was happily married to his wife, Aerope. However, their marriage might not have been as happy as Atreus thought. Thyestes, Atreus's brother, had an affair with Aerope. When Atreus discovered this, rage consumed him. He knew he would have to make Thyestes pay, and he looked toward the past for inspiration.

Atreus took two of Thyestes's boys and, like his grandfather long ago, had them murdered. He cut their flesh into tiny little pieces and mixed them in with the stew.

Unlike the Olympians, Thyestes had no way of knowing what he was being served. He ate the entire bowl, unknowingly consuming his two sons. It was only after the feast was over that he discovered what had been done.

Now, tales of Thyestes's revenge vary. Some claim that he raped his own daughter, Pelopia, since he heard a prophecy that said the child they had together—Aegisthus—would kill Atreus. Others say that because Atreus was king, he faced no consequence for his horrible deed. Because he did not die at the hands of revenge, his sons would be punished in his stead.

You might have heard of Atreus's two sons since they played prominent roles in the grandest and most famous war of all: the Trojan War.

Menelaus was one of them, and he was married to the famed Helen, whose beauty was so great that it launched a thousand ships to war. The details of the Trojan War are far more complex than that, involving intricate political alliances, vows of honor, and divine intervention. We do not have the time to go into all of it, though if this sparks your curiosity, we encourage you to learn more about this famous ten-year conflict.

For the purpose of this story, all you need to know is that the Trojan prince, Paris, with the help of Aphrodite, enchanted Helen and took her away from her home. Menelaus and his brother Agamemnon called upon their allies to bring Helen home.

The Greeks and the Trojans fought for ten years. Many good men died. Achilles was driven mad by grief after the loss of Patroclus, and he was killed by Paris's older brother, Hector. The war finally came to an end when Odysseus, Athena's favorite hero, came up with a plan that is now known as the Trojan Horse.

Menelaus brought Helen back home. The two lived happily together, though one could argue they were responsible for much suffering. However, Agamemnon was not as lucky as his brother.

Agamemnon was married to Clytemnestra, and they had three children together. Iphigenia was the eldest, Electra was the middle child, and Orestes was Agamemnon's only son and heir. He was only a baby when his father left for war.

Clytemnestra and Iphigenia accompanied Agamemnon to Troy. During the journey, Agamemnon offended the goddess Artemis by killing one of her sacred stags. As such, the goddess prevented the ships from leaving their location. Agamemnon and the rest of the Greek forces consulted the Oracle to ask how they could appease Artemis.

"You angered Artemis by killing an animal she loved," said the Oracle. "To appease her, you must sacrifice a person you love. To appease Artemis, you must kill Iphigenia."

Agamemnon tried to ask for another solution, but none was given. Clytemnestra begged for her daughter to be spared. Iphigenia did not beg. She readily accepted her fate.

Iphigenia was taken to an altar. A priestess of Artemis raised her knife, and everyone looked away. When they opened their eyes and turned back toward the altar, Iphigenia was gone. Artemis was appeased.

The Sacrifice of Iphigenia

While Agamemnon continued to Troy, Clytemnestra returned to Mycenae. While her husband was at war, she took Aegisthus, the son of Thyestes, who was born after the cannibalistic feast, as a lover. Aegisthus was determined to get revenge on Agamemnon for what his father had done to his brothers.

Agamemnon and Clytemnestra had two other children besides Iphigenia. They were Electra, another daughter, and Orestes, the only son. Electra knew of Aegisthus's plans to avenge his late brothers. While she was safe from his wicked schemes since she was a woman, she knew her baby brother would not be. And so, for this reason, she took her brother one night and sent him away to safety, someplace where Aegisthus could never get to him.

There was a time when Clytemnestra loved all of her children, but losing Iphigenia and the resentment she held toward Agamemnon soured that love. So, when Aegisthus was cruel to Electra, Clytemnestra did nothing to protect the girl. In fact, she joined in the cruelty. Young Electra endured torture and abuse for years. She took comfort in the knowledge that her little brother was safe and prayed for her father to return.

Though Electra's prayers were answered, her father's return did not bring the end of her suffering. This would come later after much blood had been spilled.

Clytemnestra met her husband outside of the palace when he returned. She had a smile on her face, and she greeted him with open arms. Though everyone knew of her affair with Aegisthus, no one had dared to warn the king of her betrayal. Thus, the weary warrior truly believed to be receiving a warm welcome.

"My husband! Oh, how long you've been away from home! How good it is to have you back!"

"I have missed you and our children dearly, Clytemnestra," Agamemnon said. "Let us enter our home and prepare a feast to celebrate my return and our victory over Troy!" Agamemnon and Clytemnestra entered the palace together.

Agamemnon brought many treasures from Troy. The city had been sacked and burned until there was nothing left. All the Trojans were forced to flee their homes. The people scattered, becoming refugees. Among Agamemnon's many prizes were concubines captured during the war. One of those concubines was the Trojan princess, Cassandra.

Cassandra was the daughter of King Priam and Queen Hecuba. She was also a priestess of Apollo and burdened with the gift of sight. All of her prophecies were fated to come true, but she was cursed to never be believed. Her warnings were never heeded. When she first saw Agamemnon's palace, she gasped in horror, fear seizing her heart.

"What is that place?" she asked. "What is that awful, awful house?"

Those around her explained that it was the palace where Agamemnon and his family lived.

But Cassandra shook her head. "No, he shall not live there," she said. "No one can live there. That is a house of blood. A house of blood and torment and suffering. So much evil has been done in that place, and there's more evil to be done still."

Tears welled in Cassandra's eyes as she stared at the house. People tried to console the fallen princess, but it was as if she could not hear them.

"Oh... Oh, I see..." she said to no one in particular. "More blood will be spilled tonight. Two more people shall die, and I shall be one of them."

Without another word, Cassandra entered the palace, never to come out again.

Hours passed. Then, Clytemnestra and Aegisthus came out of the palace, their tunics and hands stained with blood. No words were needed to explain what happened.

Clytemnestra Hesitates Before Killing the Sleeping Agamemnon by Pierre-Narcisse Guérin.
https://commons.wikimedia.org/wiki/File:Murder_of_agamemnon.jpg

"We shall remain your rulers, just as we have for the last ten years," Clytemnestra announced. "And if anyone dares to challenge our claim to the throne, they will be shown no mercy."

As you can imagine, Electra despaired at this. Her father was dead. Her mother and her lover had taken over the throne. Any hopes of having a better life now rested in the hands of a brother whom she hadn't seen since the days she could carry him in her arms.

Luckily for her, Orestes grew to be a kind, sensible, and brave young man. He was pious and humble. He was a good warrior who knew better than to be arrogant. Orestes was good friends with a young man called Pylades. The two were inseparable. Some claimed they were lovers. When word reached Orestes of what his mother had done to his father, he was struck with grief and despair. He was also caught in a dilemma.

"What shall I do, Pylades?" Orestes asked. "Our laws and traditions say I must slay the one who killed my father. It is my duty as his son. It is what the gods expect of me. But there are few greater sins than matricide. Such an act is unforgivable. So, what can I do? Do I dishonor my father by not getting revenge on him? Or do I damn my soul by killing the one who brought me into the world?"

"Yours is truly a dilemma unlike any other, and I do not envy your position, my dear Orestes," Pylades said. "I cannot advise you one way or the other. What I suggest you do is go to the Oracle of Delphi and seek the wisdom of the god Apollo himself. And know that regardless of what he says you must do, I will be forever loyal to you."

And so, Orestes and Pylades traveled to the Oracle of Delphi to seek guidance. Apollo answered Orestes's pleas.

"Your duty as a son is to your father, the one who has been wronged," said the god. "You must kill those responsible for his death. It is your duty, Orestes, son of Agamemnon, to punish Clytemnestra and Aegisthus for their wicked actions. This is your burden to bear as a member of the cursed House of Atreus."

Orestes did not rejoice at the news, but he did not try to argue. He simply bowed his head and thanked Apollo for his wisdom. With a heavy heart, sword in hand, and Pylades by his side, Orestes marched to Mycenae.

It was by chance that Orestes and Pylades ran into Electra. When they arrived in the city, Orestes declared he wished to pay his father his respects before he completed his task. Pylades accompanied him.

As soon as Electra saw Orestes, she recognized him immediately. Tears filled her eyes. When Orestes learned that this sad young woman was the sister to whom he owed his life, he embraced her and kissed her forehead.

"Oh, Orestes! My little Orestes!" cried Electra. "You are safe! You are safe! And you are here! You are home!"

"Yes, sister. I'm safe, all thanks to you. I am here, so you need not be sad anymore," Orestes said. "I'll keep you safe, and I'll ensure you feel no more misery. I'll make things right, my dearest sister."

Together, Electra, Orestes, and Pylades plotted how they could most efficiently assassinate Clytemnestra and Aegisthus.

"They know you are out there still, and now that word of Father's death has spread, they expect you to come for them at any moment," Electra said.

"We can use that to our advantage," said Pylades. "They know Orestes will come to avenge his father, but they do not know what he looks like. And they do not know we have met you, Electra. We have the upper hand."

"I hate that we must do this," Orestes said. "I hate that this is required of us. But we have no other choice. They and the gods left us no other choice. Let us just do it as quickly and painlessly as possible. There's no reason we must cause more suffering."

They agreed that Pylades and Orestes would disguise themselves as messengers. They would go to the palace and say they had important information for Clytemnestra and Aegisthus about Orestes. They would claim that Orestes was killed on his journey to Mycenae. When Clytemnestra and Aegisthus demanded to see the messengers and hear the details of what they had to say, Orestes and Pylades would take the opportunity to kill them both. Electra would stay in the palace. She would be vigilant and ensure everything worked as planned.

Wine jug depicting the murder of Aegisthus.
https://commons.wikimedia.org/wiki/File:Murder_Aegisthus_Louvre_K320.jpg

The day came to put their plot into action. Just as planned, Pylades and Orestes came bearing the news that Orestes was dead. But unlike what they had envisioned, the murderous couple came to receive the news separately. Aegisthus came first, so he was the first to be slain. Then Clytemnestra entered the room. Pylades and Orestes were ready to strike when a servant screamed out, "They lie! They lie! Orestes lives, and he is here in the palace!"

Sure enough, as Clytemnestra looked at the blood-soaked young men, she recognized one of them as her lost son. She was ready to fight him, reaching for an axe, but then something made her change her mind. Instead, she tried to plead for her life.

"I am your mother! I brought you into this world!" she cried. "Please! Please, you cannot do this to me! Please, my son. I am your only mother!"

Orestes hesitated. He could feel Pylades's and Electra's eyes on him. For a moment, he allowed himself to think of what life would be like if he spared his mother. For a moment, he thought of the woman she was before Iphigenia had been lost to them. For a moment, he grieved for a loving family that never existed.

Then, his resolve steeled.

"I am sorry, Mother," Orestes said. "Know that it is with a heavy heart that I do this. I am a member of the cursed House of Atreus, and so are you. I must doom my soul by punishing you for your wickedness. This is what the gods have decreed."

And with a swift thrust of his sword, Orestes killed Clytemnestra.

But Orestes's misfortunes did not end there. As soon as the act of matricide was complete, he saw a horrifying sight: the three Erinyes, the Furies, watched him with sharp smiles. He was a murderer now, and that made him their victim to torment and terrorize for as long as he lived.

For seven years, Orestes walked alone. The Furies followed him around, attacking him, screeching in his ears, and making his every waking moment a nightmare. He endured this torture without complaint, believing it to be his burden for murdering his mother and for being a member of the cursed House of Atreus.

One day, he went to the Temple of Delphi, seeking a place to rest. There, he met Apollo, who looked at him with pity.

"I wish I could liberate you from this torment, Orestes," Apollo said. "Alas, the power to do so is beyond me."

"I would never presume to ask such a thing of you, Lord Apollo."

"You wouldn't, would you? And that is one of the reasons why you are so underserving of this treatment," Apollo said. "Go to the Acropolis of Athens. There, my half-sister Athena shall receive you. If you make your case to her, perhaps she'll be able to give you peace."

"Are you sure I should try, my lord?"

"Would it hurt to do so?" Apollo retorted. "I cannot promise you that it will work, but I can promise you I will speak on your behalf."

And so, Orestes went to the Acropolis just as Apollo had instructed. And just as Apollo had said, Athena welcomed him and promised to hear his case. She called upon twelve judges to overlook the trial and to decide on Orestes's fate.

First, the Furies made their case. They said matricide was an unforgivable sin and that it was their duty to punish those who committed it. Orestes explained the circumstances of his actions and that he killed his mother upon Apollo's command. Apollo supported Orestes, claiming that he was responsible for the man's actions. He believed that Orestes had atoned for his cruel deed since he had spent the last seven years wandering alone and being tormented.

The judges cast their votes. Six voted in favor of Orestes. Six voted against him. It was up to Athena to decide his fate.

"You are acquitted of your charges, good Orestes," Athena said. "And not only that, I declare that due to your atonement and your humbleness, your house shall be free of the curse that has been plaguing it for generations."

If we ended our story here, we could rejoice about Orestes and his descendants finally having a chance at being happy. But this is not the end of our tale. There's one last person we must visit before all can be well.

Now, I ask you to cast your mind back to the days before the Trojan War, when Agamemnon and the other Greek forces were traveling to Troy. Do you remember how they killed one of Artemis's stags and how Iphigenia was sacrificed for their crime?

Well, some say that Artemis, the protector of maidens, would have never allowed an innocent like Iphigenia to be so cruelly slaughtered.

Instead, when the sacrifice was to be made, Artemis came down from the heavens, took the princess in her arms, and carried her to Tauris. Iphigenia was made into one of Artemis's priestesses and was kept safe at the goddess's temple.

Now, the people of Tauris were no friends to the Greeks. In fact, King Thoas decreed that every Greek who stepped on their land would be used as a human sacrifice. As Artemis's priestess, it was Iphigenia's job to prepare her own people for slaughter, cleansing them and attending to their last wishes.

"Artemis would have never wanted this. None of the gods would ever ask for human sacrifice," Iphigenia said to herself. "These are the actions of men, who are using the divine as an excuse for their barbarity."

But what choice did Iphigenia have but to go along with this? If she were revealed to be Greek, she would be sacrificed. Because she was alone, she could never fight against the people of Tauris or find a way to run back to her homeland. Her best hope of survival was to keep her head down, go along with what was expected of her, and pray that someone would come to her rescue.

Her prayers were answered one day. None other than Orestes and Pylades arrived at Tauris. This was a few years after Orestes had been freed from the Erinyes, but seven years of nonstop torment had taken a toll on his mind. Orestes was still haunted by the Furies even though they had long left him alone. Nightmares plagued his nights, and terrible visions followed him in the morning. Orestes had gone to the Oracle at Delphi to seek advice, and the Oracle ordered him to travel to Tauris and bring back the image of Artemis to Athens. Only then would he finally be able to rest in peace.

"If you are going to Tauris, then I'm going with you," said Pylades. "Nothing you can say or do will change my mind."

And so, the two set off on their journey. When they arrived at Tauris, they were immediately identified as Greeks and sent to the temple of Artemis so they could be prepared to be sacrificed.

Iphigenia did not recognize her brother, and Orestes did not recognize his sister. However, they knew each other to be Greek. As they talked while Iphigenia made the preparations for the sacrifice, they learned they both hailed from the same place.

A silver cup with Iphigenia, Pylades, and Orestes.

"You're from Mycenae as well?" Iphigenia asked, hope blossoming in her chest for the first time in years. "May I ask you a favor then?"

"Anything," said Orestes.

"How fares Agamemnon and his family?" Iphigenia asked. "I know he returned victorious from the Trojan War, but after that, word of the Greeks did not reach our shores. Tell me, what happened to him?"

Orestes and Pylades exchanged somber looks. They sighed and silently decided Orestes would break the news to this kind priestess.

"I'm afraid he is long gone," Orestes said. "Murdered by his own wife almost ten years ago."

Iphigenia sobbed. She excused herself and left the two men alone. When she came back almost an hour later, she had a letter in her hand.

"May I ask you for another favor?"

"If it is in our power to grant it, then yes," said Orestes.

"As the priestess of this temple, I can let one of you leave and escape the sacrifice, but only one," Iphigenia said. "Whichever one goes, can you deliver this letter to my brother so that he can come rescue me?"

Orestes and Pylades looked at each other again, both feeling determined.

"I'll stay," said Pylades. "You go. Take the image of Artemis to complete the quest."

But Orestes shook his head.

"No, Pylades. I will not allow you to sacrifice yourself for my sake."

"It is no sacrifice! Giving my life to spare yours is something I do willingly."

"Pylades, please. I am already tormented by the memories of the Furies and by what I have done to my mother. I could not bear to live with your death over my head too. It is my fault we are here. You were never meant to be in any danger," Orestes said. "Go. I'll stay. And look after my sister for me."

Pylades wanted to argue, but he recognized the look in his friend's eyes. He knew there was no talking him out of this. And so, with a heavy heart, he nodded and turned to Iphigenia.

"To whom should I deliver your message?"

"To Orestes, son of Agamemnon," said Iphigenia, handing Pylades the letter. "Tell him that his sister Iphigenia still lives and that she waits for him in a hostile land, eager to return home."

"Are you certain this letter should go to Orestes, son of Agamemnon?" Pylades asked, taking the letter in his hand.

"Yes. I'm certain."

Pylades looked at her, his face serious, and he spoke with the most somber of tones. "Then, Iphigenia, it will be my honor to reunite you with your brother," he said. After a beat, he turned toward Orestes. In that same tone and with that same expression, he said, "Orestes! I bring you urgent news from your sister, Iphigenia. Do you accept this letter?"

Orestes could barely contain his smile. His eyes filled with tears. As Iphigenia watched, realization dawned on her. She also started to laugh and cry.

"Yes, my dearest Pylades," Orestes said, his voice choked up. "I accept this letter. Thank you."

But instead of taking the letter, Orestes took his sister into his arms. Iphigenia hugged her little brother tightly, crying and laughing, reunited with her family at last. Pylades watched the two siblings with a smile, feeling lucky to have witnessed such a tender moment.

"Oh, look at you! My little Orestes!" Iphigenia said. "Why, you're so big! I remember when you were but a babe! You could fit in my arms and would play with my hair. But look at you now! At least a head taller than I!"

"A head taller, but I'm still your little brother who has missed you dearly," Orestes said. "But tell me, how is it that you are alive? All of us thought you long dead!"

Iphigenia filled them in on her adventures since Artemis rescued her from the sacrifice and how she ended up in Tauris.

"I am happy for both of you," said Pylades once Iphigenia was done and before more questions could be asked. "But we should save the rest of our stories for later. Right now, we must find a way to leave this place. With the image of Artemis, of course."

Orestes nodded.

"Of course. All three of us will escape." He turned toward Iphigenia. "I will not let you stay here a moment longer. You'll come with us to our ship."

And so, they schemed. During their conversation, Iphigenia learned that Orestes had committed matricide to avenge their father. She convinced Orestes and Pylades to use this as an excuse to get away from the temple.

"I've been serving here for years. King Thoas trusts me," Iphigenia said. "I'll say that I learned of your sin and that you must be purified at the ocean before you are suited to be sacrificed to the goddess. Then, we board your ship and make our escape before they realize what we've done."

"And the image of Artemis?" Pylades asked, never forgetting the reason they had come in the first place.

"We'll claim that being in your presence soiled the image and that it must be cleansed," Iphigenia responded. "But we must act quickly."

And so, they made their preparations. Iphigenia still acted as though they were getting ready to be sacrificed and tied their wrists with ropes. She grabbed the image and led them away from the temple.

Sure enough, King Thoas did not even think of questioning Iphigenia when she explained what she was doing. All those years of keeping her head down and not calling attention to herself had finally paid off.

Iphigenia could now escape without drawing suspicion.

As soon as they were out of sight, they ran to the ship. They boarded it and set sail, seeking to leave Tauris as soon as possible. Once King Thoas realized they were not returning, he set out after them. However, Athena was said to have intervened in favor of our heroes, ordering King Thoas to return to Tauris and letting Orestes, Pylades, and Iphigenia return to Mycenae.

And so, our tale finally comes to an end. The curse of the House of Atreus was lifted, and though many had suffered, Orestes, his sisters, and their descendants were able to live happy lives.

Activity 6: Family Tree

Fill in the family tree below with the names of the members of the House of Atreus.

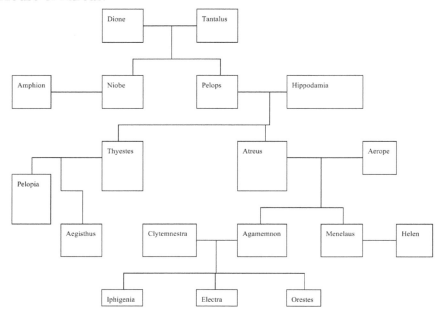

Aegisthus	Electra	Pelops	Menelaus	Tantalus	Agamemnon

Conclusion

For millennia, Greek myths have captured the imagination. Although these heroes dealt with impossible circumstances and achieved unthinkable feats, they still feel relatable. Their struggles against supernatural forces somehow make them feel achingly human. These narratives have the ability to connect those who read them, touching their humanity in ways that are hard to fully understand.

And we see these myths almost every day. There are paintings like Botticelli's *Birth of Venus* and John William Waterhouse's *Hylas and the Nymphs*. You can watch movies like Pasolini's *Medea* (1969) or Disney's *Hercules* (1997). And if books are more your style, then book series like Rick Riordan's *Percy Jackson and the Olympians* or Madeline Miller's award-winning *The Song of Achilles* and *Circe* retellings have you covered. There are video games like Supergiant Games' *Hades,* the musical *Hadestown,* and webcomics like Rachel Smythe's *Lore Olympus.* These stories have always been and will always be prominent in artistic expression and entertainment.

While this book offers but a small fraction of what Greek mythology has to offer, we hope that we have entertained and inspired you. If you have enjoyed your journey so far, we encourage you to seek out more myths, such as the ones about the Trojan War, the Odyssey, the Theban Cycle, and Orpheus and Eurydice. Our bibliography also serves as a great list of other resources you can use to further expand your knowledge and dive deeper into the wonderful world of Greek myths.

Free limited time bonus

Stop for a moment. We have a free bonus set up for you. The problem is this: we forget 90% of everything that we read after 7 days. Crazy fact, right? Here's the solution: we've created a printable, 1-page pdf summary for this book that you're reading now. All you have to do to get your free pdf summary is to go to the following website: **https://livetolearn.lpages.co/enthrallinghistory/**

Once you do, it will be intuitive. Enjoy, and thank you!

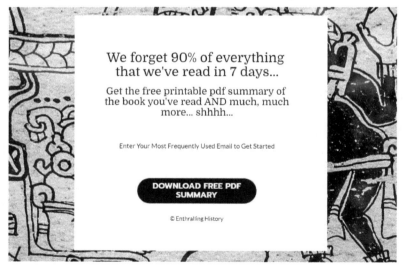

Further Reading

Bulfinch, Thomas. 1867. *Bulfinch's Mythology.* 2013. New York: Barnes and Noble Books.

Fry, Stephen. 2017. *Mythos: The Greek Myths Reimagined.* San Francisco: Chronicles Book.

Hamilton, Edith. 1942. *Mythology.* 2012. Boston: Little, Brown and Company.

Illes, Judika. 2009. *Encyclopedia of Spirits: The Ultimate Guide to the Magic of Fairies, Genies, Demons, Ghosts, Gods & Goddesses.* New York: Harper One.

John, Judith, Christopher McNab, and K.E Sullivan. 2013. "Classical Greek." In *Myths and Legends,* edited by Jake Jackson, 191-266. New York: Flame Tree Publishing.

Roman, Luke, and Monica Roman. 2010. *Encyclopedia of Greek and Roman Mythology.* New York: Facts on File.

Answer Key

Activity 1: Matching Activity

Match the names in Column A with the correct attributes in Column B

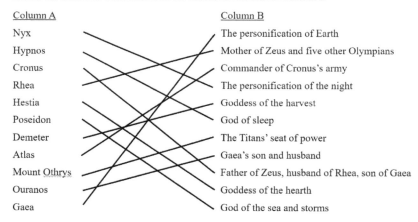

Column A

Nyx
Hypnos
Cronus
Rhea
Hestia
Poseidon
Demeter
Atlas
Mount Othrys
Ouranos
Gaea

Column B

The personification of Earth
Mother of Zeus and five other Olympians
Commander of Cronus's army
The personification of the night
Goddess of the harvest
God of sleep
The Titans' seat of power
Gaea's son and husband
Father of Zeus, husband of Rhea, son of Gaea
Goddess of the hearth
God of the sea and storms

Activity 2: Multiple Choice

Answer the questions below.

1. Who designed the Labyrinth?

   b) Daedalus

2. What did Ariadne give Theseus to help him escape?

   d) Silver thread

3. What are the two main cities of this tale?

    a) Crete and Athens

4. Which deity gave the Cretan Bull to Minos?

    c) Poseidon

5. Who are the parents of the Minotaur?

    d) Pasiphae and the Cretan Bull

6. How many tributes were sent to the Labyrinth each time?

    d) Seven boys and seven maidens

Activity 3: Open-close Exercise

In each sentence, circle the correct answer.

1. Perseus was the son of **Zeus**/*Poseidon* and the mortal princess Danae.
2. When Danae and Perseus arrived at Seriphos, *Polydectes*/**Dictys** welcomed them into his home.
3. Medusa was cursed by *Poseidon*/**Athena** to have snake hair that would turn whoever looked at her into stone.
4. To aid him in his quest, Athena and **Hermes**/*Aphrodite* and Zeus gave Perseus *poison arrows, a club, and a golden thread*/**a mirrored shield, winged sandals, and the helm of darkness**.
5. Andromeda, daughter of **Cepheus**/*Phineus* and Cassiopeia, was the princess of *Argos*/**Aethiopia**.
6. After defeating Polydectes, Perseus, Andromeda, and Danae left Seriphos for **Argos**/*Larissa*.

Activity 4: Timeline

Number Herakles's twelve labor in the correct order.

(06) Slay the Stymphalian Birds

(03) Capture Artemis's Ceryneian Hind

(09) Retrieve Hippolyta's Belt

(01) Slay and skin the Nemean Lion

(11) Steal three golden apples from the Hesperides' garden

(12) Bring Cerberus to the mortal realm alive

(02) Slay the Lernaean Hydra

(05) Clean the Augean Stables

(10) Bring Geryon's Cattle

(07) Capture the Cretan Bull

(04) Capture the Erymanthian Boar alive

(08) Steal the Mares of Diomedes

Activity 5: Fill-in-the-blank Exercise

Fill in the blank spots with the correct answer from the box below.

1. The Oracle warned Pelias to beware of the **Man with One Sandal**.

2. The zodiac constellation of **Aries** is based on the golden ram that saved the twins Phrixus and Helle from being sacrificed by their stepmother.

3. The ship Jason and his crew journeyed on was called the **Argo**, and for this reason, they were known as the **Argonauts**.

4. Herakles's lover, **Hylas**, was taken by Naiads.

5. Jason passed through the **Symplegades** by first releasing a dove. After seeing how fast they clashed, he knew at what speed to row.

6. **Aeetes** was the king of Colchis. He had three children: **Chalciope**, **Medea**, and **Absyrtus**.

7. To help Jason steal the Golden Fleece, Medea put **the dragon** to sleep.

8. Orpheus saved the crew from certain death at the hands of the **Sirens** by playing his lyre and singing.

9. The **Talos** was a gigantic bronze automaton created by Hephaestus and gifted to Minos to guard his island against pirates and invaders.

10. When Jason betrayed Medea to marry Glauce, Medea got her revenge by cursing a **cloak** and a **crown** that were given to the couple as wedding gifts.

Activity 6: Family Tree

Fill in the family tree below with the names of the members of the House of Atreus.

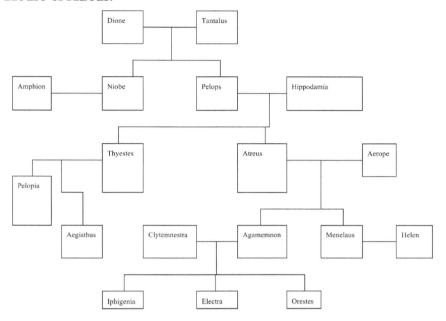

Milton Keynes UK
Ingram Content Group UK Ltd.
UKHW020626071223
433866UK00006B/155